Fishing Soft Plastics For Bass

Tips and Patterns

Mike Mladenik

Northwoods Guide

CONTENTS

Chapter 1   The Plastic Worm ………………………8
Chapter 2   Grubs……………………………………..24
Chapter 3   Skirted Grubs……………………………43
Chapter 4   Tubes……………………………………...62
Chapter 5   Wacky Worms & Stick Baits…………..81
Chapter 6   Jerkbaits………………………………….101
Chapter 7   Slider Fishing…………………………..113
Chapter 8   Mojo Rigs………………………………125
Chapter 9   Drop Shot……………………………...134
Chapter 10   Shaky Head Fishing…………………..144
Chapter 11   Doodling…..……………………………152
Chapter 12   Carolina Rigs……………….…..………158
Chapter 13   Creature Baits & other Plastic Baits….166

Introduction

Soft plastics have had an incredible journey form their original beginnings in the late 1940's in the Akron, Ohio basement of Nick Crème. While the "Plastic Worm" looks crude at best by today's standards it started a revolution in the fishing tackle industry.

My introduction to soft plastics began in the mid 1960's at a small quarry a few miles from my home. As a kid I would spend countless hours trying to figure out fish and was content even if I did not catch anything. Soft plastics opened up a whole new world and I never looked back. If I would have spent one tenth as much time on my schoolwork my life might have turned out differently. However, then I would not be fishing every day!

My passion for fishing and a corresponding distaste for urban environments led me to the northwoods where I have spent over 30 years as a professional guide. Soft plastics are a dream come true for a bass guide; they are inexpensive and user friendly. On many occasions, reaching into my bag of tricks has enabled a client with limited expertise to fish like a pro.

In the northwoods anglers are blessed with an endless supply of water with varied and diverse fisheries. Here is where I found my niche for smallmouth bass. I quickly realized that smallmouth relate to habitat differently on a deep clear natural lake than on a stained water reservoir. I also learned that regardless of the type of water they inhabit, smallmouth bass will strike a properly placed soft plastic bait.

A guide does not have the option of only fishing when the weather is perfect and the fish are biting. Based on the hands-on day to day experiences of a northwoods fishing guide with over 40,000 hours on the water, this book will unlock a few secrets for anglers who fish soft plastics in northern waters. Even anglers who fish southern or western reservoirs will find a few tips that will help when the bite is tough.

Today we have plastic worms, finesse worms, floating worms, sinking worms, tubes, jerkbaits, grubs, sweat beavers, reaper tails, pre-rigged worms, skirted grubs and wacky worms just to name a few. On any given day, they can all catch a load of bass. The challenge is for the angler to figure out which bait and what color will be the ticket for that particular day and the type of water they are fishing. I truly hope that by sharing my experiences the angler will better understand the big picture and learn how to put the pieces of the puzzle together.

I have been fortunate to make my living on the water, and fortunate to have been along for the ride for a good portion of the soft plastic revolution. One can only imagine the future of these wonderful lures. Bass beware!

Chapter 1
The Plastic Worm

    Most collectors and historians are in agreement that the first legitimate plastic worm had its beginnings in the late 1940's in an Akron, Ohio basement. There are some reports of forerunner "rubber" worms, but it is Nick and Cosma Creme who are credited with molding the first "plastic" worm and launching it on the market as we know it today.

    Akron was the hub of the rubber and chemical industry. Although Nick Crème was a machinist by trade, he had access to people and formulas that led him to the development of the plastic worm. These early worms had three-hook harnesses threaded through their bellies to emulate a crawler harness. While there were plenty of hard baits on the market, if you wanted to catch bass consistently you fished with a live nightcrawler. So with this in mind Nick Creme invented the first hand poured worms.

The Creme Lure Company made its debut at the 1950 Cleveland, Ohio, boat show where curious anglers snatched up 9,600 "Wiggle Worms" with a package of five worms selling for a whopping $1. The rest is history. It quickly caught on in the Midwest and by the early 1950's the new Creme Scoundrel worms were beginning to pop up across the south. About that time the newly developed reservoirs in the south were beginning to provide outstanding bass fishing. Anglers were discovering that those flooded trees and brushpiles harbored a lot of bass and the plastic worm was the ideal bait to catch them.

Local anglers were quick to make modifications to the plastic worm in order to adapt to southern reservoirs. In the late 1950's, Creme noticed his company was shipping numerous baits to the Tyler, Texas, area and that requests for replacement worms without the three-hook harnesses were skyrocketing. He soon discovered that Texas anglers were using his replacement worms on Lake Tyler, which opened a few years earlier. When fishing on Lake Tyler anglers were threading a single hook through the Scoundrel's head, rotating the hook and then buried the barb into the body to guard against snagging in the wood. Lake Tyler is where the first Texas rig was fished, but nobody knows who the angler was that is responsible for creating it. Surely he intended to keep the Texas rigged worm a secret.

Once Crème discovered that anglers throughout Texas were falling in love with the plastic worm and the Texas rig that they were using on other brush-filled lakes, he had to get in on the action. That prompted him to move his business to Tyler in 1960, capitalizing on the growing plastic worm market. Interestingly, the move occurred around the same time Skeeter was building the first fiberglass bass boat 24 miles up the road. The bass fishing revolution had begun and the plastic worm was an important player.

There was one problem with the Creme worm, anglers would buy them but most fishermen did not know how to use them. The guys who were catching all the bass were very tight lipped. Most anglers would fish them like a real nightcrawler, letting the bass swallow the worm before they set the hook. This method worked fine but it led to high bass mortality. There was no catch and release back then so even if the bass did not swallow the plastic worm it would end up on a stringer anyway. However, there probably were many bass that were released but never survived.

Nick Creme

It did not take long before other companies popped up throughout the Southwest. Fliptail Lures made the first plastic worm that was made by injecting plastic into a mold. Fliptail also is said to have made the first plastic lizard. They have long been out of production but molds are available for anglers who pour their own worms.

Tom Mann impregnated his worm with fruity scents in a much softer plastic. Mann was perhaps the first one to use "scented" baits in mass production, as his variety of plastic worms were packaged in different colors with such fragrances as blueberry, strawberry, and watermelon just to name a few. Credited with discovering and manufacturing the famous "Mann's Jelly Worm", the legendary Alabama angler and entrepreneur started Mann's Bait Company in 1958. In addition to the famous jelly worms, he molded a piece of lead and attached a treble hook and spinner to it for casting deep depths where big bass resided in summer months. The business grew into a multimillion-dollar company when he sold it in 1979. Mann's jelly worms became my personal favorites over the years and when I am fishing for largemouth bass you can find one on the end of my line.

Mann's Jelly Worm

As the plastic worm phenomenon swept across the country, anglers discovered that a Texas rigged worm could be fished easily in grass and wood. They seemed to be catching bass no matter where they were fished. There were even rumors of people wanting to ban the plastic worm in some states because they caught too many fish. Most of this was probably the grumbling of live bait fisherman who did not want to admit that an artificial worm could out fish their beloved nightcrawler.

In the "60's, for the most part the angler had very limited color selection with black, grape and red being the staples. Due to the demands of anglers, manufacturers began to make requested colors for regional waters. In the early days if a bass did not hit a black, grape, or red worm anglers just assumed the bass weren't biting. Nobody ever thought of matching the worms' color to the clarity of the water. Today, with a multiple of colors from which to choose, anglers will often change color before a bass gets a chance to adjust to it.

During the early years improvements in the texture of the worm were slow to come by. The original worms were either hard, which made it difficult to set a hook, or too soft, which allowed the hook point to penetrate too easily and therefore snags were often a problem. Eventually the proper consistency was reached, being soft enough to give the worm action but durable enough to be fished in heavy cover.

In the early years of worm fishing, most anglers paid little attention to their equipment and just pitched a plastic worm on their favorite bass rod. The angler would make what he thought was the perfect cast but after a few turns of the reel the worm would get hung up in the brush. When this occurred to me, like many anglers I would blame the poor quality of the worm. Little did I know it was in my choice of rod. Wanting to "feel the fight" I used a wimpy rod and once a worm was hung, I could not pull it out of the cover. Eventually, like most worm fishermen, I switched to better quality rods that had plenty of backbone to handle the cover and a big bass.

Today the preferred worm rod is a medium to medium heavy action, six and a half feet in length with a limber tip. The limber tip is needed for casting the lighter weight Texas rigged worm. The medium heavy action will give the rod the backbone necessary to drive the hook through the worm and into the jaw of the bass. Team this rod with a high speed bait casting reel that has a 6:1 retrieve ratio. The high speed reel allows you to get your bait in quickly when you need to make another cast to your target. When fishing a plastic worm on a bait caster, I spool my reel with 12-17 pound monofilament if I am in heavy cover. I use a bullet shaped slip sinker most of the time when worm fishing since it allows the sinker to slide freely up and down the line. The reason behind this is it reduces the potential of the fish throwing the bait when they jump. If I am fishing heavier cover then I will "Peg" the sinker to the head of the worm. There are a couple ways that you can "Peg" a worm. One is by forcing a tooth pick into the bottom hole of the sinker. The only problem with this is that you run the risk of damaging your line. A few manufacturers make specialty products out of rubber and they pull through the sinker holding it in place without damaging your line.

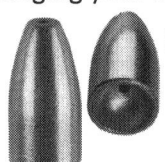 **Bullet sinker**

Screw type sinker

One alternative to pegging the sinker is to use a screw type sinker. This is often called the Florida Rig where the sinker has a small spring molded into the bottom of a bullet sinker. The line slips through the sinker just as a regular slip sinker and then the sinker is screwed onto the head of the worm to secure the whole rig together. There must be about one quarter inch of the worm head above the eye of the hook for this rig to work properly. The disadvantage of the Florida Rig is it causes the head of the worm to be torn up more often due to the spring being inserted into the worm. While an angler may go through more worms the advantages out weight the cost of a few more worms.

As far as choosing a worm hook I use 1/0-2/0-3/0-4/0 and 5/0 wide gap hooks depending on the size of the worm and the type of cover I'm fishing. Be sure that you don't overpower the baits you are using with hooks that are too large. Hooks are manufactured in "Light Wire" and "Heavy Wire". A good rule of thumb when selecting the right hook is (1) Heavy cover/structure-Heavy Line-Heavy Plastic baits...Heavy Wire Hooks. (2) Spinning tackle with lighter line and lighter baits...Light Wire Hooks.

Worm Hooks

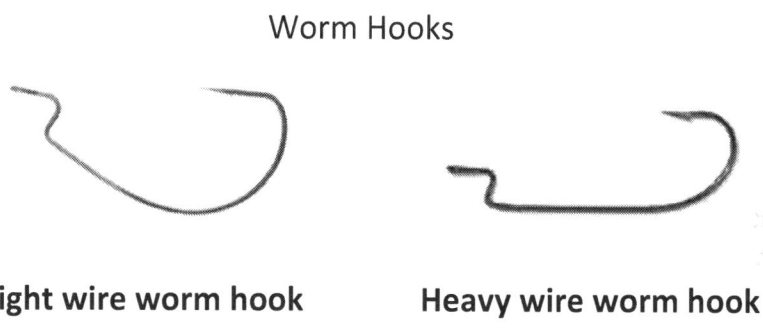

Light wire worm hook   **Heavy wire worm hook**

Worm color will depend on the clarity of the water you are fishing. In clear water use Green pumpkin, pumpkin, root beer, black and black/blue. In clear water I prefer a straight tailed worm since they fall faster and the fish can see them easily.

In stained water use watermelon red, purple, black, black/fire tail and red. Curly tail worms are great in stained water.

In murky or muddy water try red, June bug, chartreuse, electric purple and electric blue. In muddy water opt for a fatter ribbon tailed worm that will produce more underwater vibrations which the fish will feel many times before they can see them.

What size worm to choose will depend on the season, water clarity and geographic location. In spring a four inch worm is best for clear water northern lakes but in muddy water an eight inch worm could be the ticket south of the Mason-Dixon Line. Generally the clearer the water the smaller the worm should be in spring; be sure to increase the size of the worm as the water temperature rises. In summer, it is also a good idea to downsize your worm after a cold front.

Cast the worm towards some sort of shoreline cover or structure and let it fall to the bottom. You will be able to tell when it has reached the bottom when the line goes slack. Pay close attention to the line as it falls because frequently the bass will hit the worm as it descends.

Once your bait is resting on the bottom, reel up the slack line and give the tip a couple little twitches. If this does not produce a strike, begin to slowly hop the worm along the bottom or over the structure you are fishing. It is not necessary to move the rod tip a great deal to produce an effective movement of the worm. Generally I do not move the rod more than 6- to 8-inches. Granted, the amount of movement needed will be determined by the type of area you are fishing.

During your retrieve it is very vital to pay attention to your line. Should the line go slack all of a sudden chances are the worm is in the mouth of a bass. It is also very common for the line to begin to move sideways. This occurs when a bass picks up the bait and swims perpendicular to the direction of your cast. Should this occur, reel up any slack line and set the hook.

When fishing a plastic worm I try to bounce the worm off of everything possible to attract a bass. It is important to keep your rod directly in front of you at a 45 degree angle. At times I will move the worm slowly along the bottom while at other times I will retrieve it with a "twitch," giving it an erratic movement. Keep focused on what the worm is doing. Sometimes the bite will be vicious, at other times it will be ever so light. But when you detect a bite reel the slack out of your line and set the hook. When you set a hook with a plastic worm rigged Texas style, give it all you've got!

Flipping and Pitching are two deadly techniques for fishing plastic worms but beginning anglers can easily get them confused. Pitching is a long distance version of flipping. Most anglers use an underhand flip cast when pitching, keeping the bait as close to the water as possible. This method is awesome when the fish are very shallow and you want to avoid spooking the fish by getting too close to them. At times you may have to make several long pin point pitches to the same spot while crawling the bait back towards you. Once again, concentration is critical at all times. This method allows you to fish thick cover that might be unfishable in any other manner.

On the other hand, when flipping you get as close to the fish as possible. You make far shorter flips and you are working the bait up and down in a vertical manner as you climb your bait through the limbs and branches. Once again, watch your line and keep up your concentration.

**Northwoods largemouth caught with a
Texas rigged plastic worm**

Plastics are normally rigged in a Texas rig manner and sinkers are pegged against the head of the worm. When flipping use a 7 1/2ft or 8ft heavy action rod, a 6:3:1 bait casting reel and 25lb test line.

Fishing a floating plastic worm is yet another useful technique and it is quite easy to learn and a lot of fun. The visual strikes this method produces at times are breath taking. Floating worms or trick worms can be fished on bait casters or spinning gear equally as well. One major key to fishing this method correctly is finding out what the fish want. At times they want a floating worm that is moving like a snake and at other times they want bait that is moving slow and easy. To rig a "Floating Worm" you attach the hook in the same manner as a Texas rigged worm but without a weight. There is really no wrong way to fish a floating worm.

On a few occasions I have fished floating worms and have been impressed. They work especially well when fished over submerged milfoil. I found this pattern on a stained water reservoir that I fish and it is consistent during the post-spawn. After largemouth spawn they will move off the beds and head into the milfoil to feed. Largemouth will scatter throughout the milfoil but they are a bit sluggish from spawning. I will slowly twitch the floating worm with an occasional pause over the milfoil. The strikes are savage. Largemouth won't hit a topwater bait on this particular reservoir during the post-spawn but they like the floating worm.

While I still use my share of Texas rigged plastic worms, with so many new things on the market it is easy to forget about the lure that started the revolution in soft plastics.

How to Texas Rig a Plastic Worm

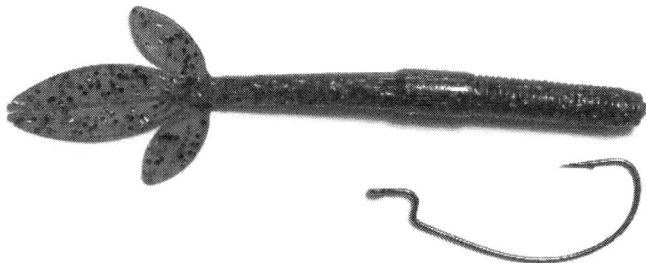

Slip a bullet sinker onto your line by inserting the line into the pointed end of the sinker. Tie a wide gap offset worm hook onto the line.

Insert about ¼ of an inch of the point of the hook straight into the top of the worm. Turn the hook point and exit the worm at the side of the head.

Slide the worm up the hook toward the eye, twisting it around the hook wire as you slide it, so that the point of the hook will be facing the worm.

The eye of the hook should be just at the top of the worm. The oddest should hold the main wire of the hook outside the worm so the worm can hang straight down toward the point.

Bend the worm so that you can insert the point of the hook into the worm at a right angle. Make sure you keep the worm straight so the hook is going back into the same side of the worm that it came out of.

Push the point all the way through the worm. When you are done doing this, the worm should make a straight line between the point and the eye of the hook. Next push up on the worm just a little so you can slip the point of the hook just under the surface of the plastic to "skin-hook the worm". A worm rigged like this will be weedless but still allow for an easy hookset.

Plastic Worms

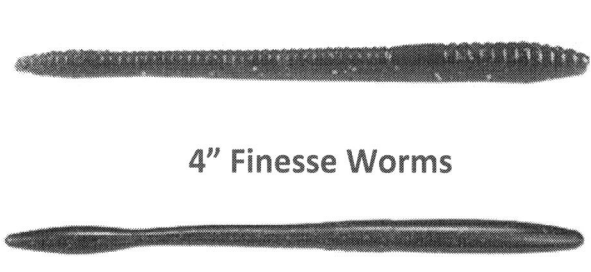

4" Finesse Worms

Finesse worms. These plastic worms are thin, short worms of 3 to 4 inches (7.5 to 10 cm), designed to fish with light tackle in clear water conditions, such as those found in older reservoirs that have lost most of their grass and sunken timber cover. They are often fished with light split shot or "Slider" jig heads.

Straight-tail Worm

Straight-tail worms. These worms, usually 6 inches (15 cm) in length, resemble nightcrawlers in appearance, usually in everything but color. These worms are usually retrieved straight, although they can also be fished in a "lift-and-drop" style.

Paddle-tail worms

Paddle-tail worms. These worms feature longer segments and a tail that looks like the business end of a paddle or oar. These worms are often fished with a straight retrieve. Paddle-tail worms are usually around 7 inches (17.5 cm) in length, although jumbo version may exceed 10 inches (25 cm).

Forked-tail Worm

Forked-tail worms. These worms come in the same lengths and are segmented like paddle-tail worms, but they feature a forked tail instead of a paddle tail.

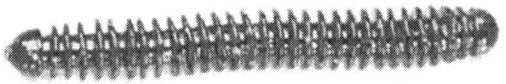

French-fry Worm

French-fry worms. These worms have pronounced segments like that of a crinkle-cut French fry or of a centipede or caterpillar. These segments create resistance when the worm is drawn through the water, producing an erratic swimming motion.

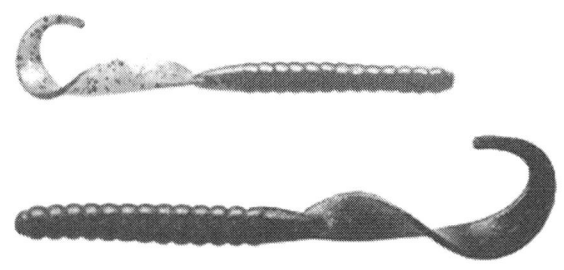

Ribbon-tail Worms

Ribbon-tail/ripple-tail worms. These worms may be segmented near the head like either straight-tail or paddle-tail worms, but they feature a curved tail section that ripples or waves like a ribbon when the worm is drawn through the water. Some plastic worms of this type feature little more than a hook-like tail, while others devote 1/2 to 2/3 of the worm's length to the curved tail; some feature 2 or more tail curls. These worms are usually fished in low-visibility conditions or in underwater cover, but they may also be fished in open water as an alternative to finesse or straight-tail worms. Some styles of this type of worm have a tendency to hang up in submerged brush, which some anglers try to prevent by liberally coating the worm with scented oils.

Gator-tail Worm

This worm is best in shallow water, especially during summer and early autumn, and it's also one of the most productive lures for river systems. This worm is best fished with a 3/16- or 1/4-ounce sinker to make the tail work properly. Let it drop straight to the bottom, then pick it up so the tail spins, then drop it again. The slow tail action that lets it swim like a lazy shad, so that's how you want to use it. Just swim it over and around cover. It's a good night fishing lure, too, because it presents a large silhouette.

Curly-tail Worm

Curly-tail worms exhibit action from their tails as a curly tail grabs more water slowing the lures fall. They have less action than a ribbon-tail worm or gator-tail worm. The slower fall and tail action puts out a little more vibration tan a straight-tail worm and is more likely to visually attract active and moderately active bass. Remember, bass are primarily sight feeders and worms as a rule make no significant sound.

5" Case Paddle Jack

Case Jacks Worm

Chapter 2
Grubs

Each year there is a new soft plastic bait on the market and like every other bass angler I can't wait to try one out on my favorite honey hole. Maybe this new hot bait will work or maybe after a few attempts it will be filed with the odd assortment of tackle in the back of my truck or simply tossed on one of my many bait piles scattered in my office or basement never to be fished again. When I try out a new bait I could pick the wrong day to fish this new hot bait or perhaps come to the conclusion that it just won't work on my favorite Northwoods lake. After all, there is no such thing as a lure that will catch bass regardless of where you live, the type of water or the weather conditions; or is there? If I had to choose one artificial bait for catching smallmouth and largemouth bass on any given body of water regardless of the weather conditions or season it would have to be a grub.

A grub is nothing more than a long slender chunk of plastic with a curly or straight tail, or as many anglers refer to them, "a jig and twister tail". The Mister Twister Curly Tail grub was created in a small town when a fisherman using a pressure cooker melted down old plastic and melted it into book molds. Prior to the development of the curly tail grub in 1972 plastic lures were worms or grubs with little or no action and they were hard to the touch. Although curly tail grubs have been around for a long time they will still catch bass consistently.

Mister Twister curly tail grub

However, in recent years due to all the new innovations in plastics they have taken a back seat and many younger bassers don't even know they exist. At times, grubs are the only thing that works and there have been many days on the water when if I would have switched to grubs earlier in the day, my success rate would have been much higher.

Although grubs will catch bass spring, summer and fall, many anglers fail to understand their versatility and how to use them effectively. It is common for anglers to take a grub out of their tackle box, rig it on any old jighead or hook and just start casting. Sure, on occasion they'll catch a bass, but most of the time they will get the grub hung up on a rock or tree, break it off and tie on a different bait. Many of todays anglers just don't have the patience to master the fine art of fishing with grubs.

I must confess that I had a long love affair with grubs and started using them before I moved to the northwoods. There was a small quarry a few miles from my home where the neighborhood people would go to wet a line. The quarry was easily accessible with plenty of good places to fish from shore and it had a good fish population. Most of the people would toss out a bobber and a worm hoping to catch anything that would bite. Usually the catch of the day was a mess of sunfish and the occasional largemouth bass. While soaking a bobber and catching small sunfish was great, after a while it did become too easy.

Since I was bored with catching sunfish it was time to figure out how to catch the largemouth bass in the quarry on something other than a worm and a bobber. Not that there is anything wrong with fishing with a worm and a bobber but I always had this urge to look for different ways to catch fish. I would spend countless hours trying to figure out fish and was content even if I did not catch anything. If I would have spent one tenth as much time on my schoolwork my life might have turned out differently. However, then I would not be fishing every day!

When I graduated high School back in 1972 I started working on construction and carried a few fishing rods in my car. While I fished many places, I continued to spend as much time as possible at the quarry where I cut my teeth. Catching these quarry bass was not easy since the quarry was heavily fished and all the good spots were taken. If I saw somebody catch a bass on a particular bait I walked over to check out what kind of lure they were using.

One evening after work, I saw a guy casting what I thought was a yellow plastic worm. After I watched him catch a huge bass I ran over to him to study the bass but I was more interested in that yellow plastic worm on which he had caught the bass. After the man released the big bass, which was unheard of in those days, he gladly showed me the bait and explained to me that it was a leadhead jig and a yellow "Mister Twister" tail. The man said that the water in the quarry is murky so yellow was the best color. I also remembered that he said that he had just got back from Canada where the water was clear and that black was the best color.

After I got my degree in color selection it was time to show me how to thread the twister tail on the jighead so the twister tail would sit straight on the hook. One point he stressed was that if the twister tail was not rigged straight on the hook, it would not catch as many fish. If I had not seen that guy catch the big bass I wouldn't have paid any attention to his advice. However, it was the biggest bass I had ever seen and I would have believed anything he had told me.

Next, he showed me how to cast out the bait and slowly reel in the lure. The trick was to find the proper retrieve. If you worked the bait too fast the bass would not hit the bait and if you worked it too slow you would get hung up in the weeds or on the bottom. It did require a bit of concentration. I asked him where I could get myself one and the guy gave me two jig and twister tails already rigged up.

I never saw that guy again but he had opened my eyes to a whole new world. No more using baits with treble hooks that continuously got snagged in the weeds and seldom caught any bass in this small quarry. The jig and twister tail would also pick up its share of weeds, but once I learned how to fish the jig and twister tight to the weeds as slowly as possible I had a good chance of catching a bass. A few of my friends tried this but they did not have the patience to finesse the jig and grub. This was my first experience with fishing a grub and it would not be my last. I guess this was one adult that did know how to fish. It of course helped that I realized at an early age the importance of listening to people who were older than me.

After I figured out how to catch these bass on a consistent basis I also figured out that if I released the bass I could come back the next day and catch it again. So at an early age I became an advocate of catch and release and I would get ticked when the adults would put the bass into their buckets.

While that small quarry introduced me to the world of the largemouth bass and how to use finesse presentations I soon graduated to strip pits. Strip pits are coal strip mines that filled up with water and either accidentally or intentionally were stocked with a variety of species of fish including largemouth bass. How the largemouth bass got into the strip pits is irrelevant, but one thing is for certain they were home to big largemouth bass. What attracted my friends and I to these pits was the few hot tips we had about huge largemouth bass being caught there.

Fishing these strip pits would be my first real challenge and was one of the best learning experiences I have ever experienced. Unlike the small quarry that had plenty of weeds and shoreline cover, the water in the strip pits was extremely clear and there were no weeds at all.
To make matters worse, the shorelines surrounding the pits were very steep crushed rock tailings void of any vegetation or cover. As far as I could tell these pits were just deep holes with the only cover being an occasional small point made up of rock tailings and submerged old mining equipment.

There were a few places where you could easily fish from shore and they attracted the most anglers and, of course, fishing pressure. The popular fishing pattern was to cast out one rod with a nightcrawler on a bottom rig and with another rod cast a Rapala or spinnerbait. Usually the guy casting the Rapala or spinnerbait would catch one or two nice bass right away but the action quickly died and within a short time everyone would be sitting on the bank watching their bottom rig. While the bottom rig would occasionally produce a big bass, they were few and far between. I knew that there had to be a ton of bass in the pit I just had to figure out how to get to them.

We did not have any boats and even if we did, it would have been impossible to find a place to drag one into the water. I just would have to hoof it along the banks like a mountain goat. When you are young you can walk along a steep bank until you find a one foot section of flat rock or tailings and start casting. Beside my legs being in prime shape, I also relied heavily on my eyesight. Due to the gin clear water I could see the bass suspending over open water, many times within easy casting distance of the shore. While I did not have any idea as to the actual depth at which the bass were suspending, I knew that the only lure that I had that would get into the strike zone was a grub.

Yes, that same jig and twister tail that I used to catch bass in that small quarry also worked in the strip pits. However, I quickly came to the conclusion that bass did not like a bright yellow twister tail in the gin clear water. Back in those days, the early 1970's, long before Bass Pro Shop, when you went into a store that sold fishing tackle your selection of colors was slim. I had to settle on two colors, black and purple, and knew that I would have to make them work.

My first attempt at fishing grubs at the strip pits was a success because I caught more bass than my friends. I only caught one bass, but it was the only fish of the day. I knew I was on to something but I also knew I had to refine my presentation. My biggest problem was that I was not casting my grub as far as I had wanted. I knew that I would have to figure out how to get more distance out of my casting. One thing was for certain, the five foot six inch rod and ten pound test line would have to go.

I was working as a construction laborer right out of High School thus having money to spend, so I headed to a new sport shop that had opened not far from my home. I had read in a magazine about using light line and was going to buy a new rod and reel combo. After spending over an hour in the place I finally settled on a six foot six rod, a new Mitchel 300 and six pound test line. I also found a large selection of grubs and jigheads and loaded up.

On Saturday all my friends had plans so I decided to make the 50 mile trip to the strip pits alone. I found the place deserted and it was a perfect time to try out my new rod and collection of grubs. The first thing I did was rig up a ¼ ounce black leadhead jig and a purple four inch curly tail grub. I put the rest of my jigheads and grubs into a small burlap sack and stuck it in my back pocket. I started walking the shoreline and it did not take long for me to locate a large school of bass cruising open water.

I firmly planted my feet knowing that if I slipped into the water I would be in trouble since the steep bank plummeted into deep water and I was alone. However, there were a ton of bass out there and I was going to catch them. My first cast went off smooth and I easily casted my new rig 50 percent farther than my old rig. I let the grub sink for about twenty seconds and started a slow steady retrieve. After about a dozen casts I decided to change my grub since I knew that those bass were still out there.

I figured that I needed to change grub color, the size of my jighead or both. Next, I reached into my sack and tied on a 3/8 ounce black jighead and a four inch black grub. After my cast I counted to 30 letting the grub drop well into the water column. I gave the grub a slight jerk and started my slow steady retrieve. After retrieving the grub about 10 feet I felt a steady pull on the line and a big bass broke water.

While I was fighting the bass my feet suddenly became uncomfortable. I looked down to see my feet and noticed that the water was over the toes of my work shoes. There was nothing I could do but keep fighting the bass even though I did not have a net nor could I bend over to grab it or even hope to beach it. So here I was trapped in the wet gravel with a big bass on the line. Eventually I horsed the big bass to the shoreline and needless to say either my knot or the line broke. I can't verify how big the bass was but in my mind it was at least seven or eight pounds.

I was still stuck in the gravel and instead of trying to get out; I reached into my bag and tied on another 3/8 ounce black leadhead jig with a four inch black curly tail grub. After repeating my previous presentation I connected with another bass although I immediately knew it was a smaller fish. This bass must have weighted about two pounds and I easily pulled it out of the water, unhooked it and released it.

All I was thinking about was that there were more bass out there. I paid no attention to the fact that I was sliding into the strip pit. I was pondering whether I caught the bass due to my heavier jig which dropped deeper into the water column or the fact that I switched grub color. After my sixth bass I knew I had to address my problem but I was afraid to move figuring that I would surly slide into the strip pit.

I tried to pull my foot out of the gravel and before I knew it my butt was stuck in the gravel. I guess I was lucky I had a few extra pounds on me since a skinny guy would have more than likely slid completely into the pit. I suddenly realized that during all the commotion my rod had slipped out of my hands. I looked into the strip pit and saw my new rod and reel wedged on a rock. About three feet from the rod I noticed my burlap sack also sitting atop a rock.

My fishing was over for the day and I rolled over on my belly grabbed a rock and pulled myself out of the water. It took a while but I eventually pulled myself up to a spot where I could stand up and hike up to the top of the tailing pile. Once I reached the top of the pile I looked down and in the clear water I could see my rod and reel, burlap bag and a big school of bass. Talk about adding insult to injury.

The next week I went back to the sports shop and bought the same rod and reel combo along with a selection of grubs. The guy at the shop asked "Didn't you buy that same combo last week?"

I replied, "Yes, and I liked it so much I decided to buy another one. I caught a bunch of big bass on those black grubs and I better stock up on them." There was no way I was going to tell him that the rod is now stuck on a rock in that strip pit.

I continued to fish that particular strip mine but I was not quite as adventurous. It did become my testing area for experimenting with different grubs, jigheads and fishing line. I have shared this observation with many of my clients over the years and it's true: if you can catch fish consistently out of a strip pit you can catch bass out of any clear water natural lake.

Once I started to fish in the northwoods, I found clear water natural lakes everywhere. The best part about these lakes is that many of them were loaded with smallmouth bass. Not that I have anything against fishing for largemouth bass, except why would I fish for them when I had lakes full of smallmouth. For many years, I would start using grubs on clear water natural lakes as soon as I hit the water. At that time, water temperatures were in the upper forties to low fifties.

I rely heavily on a three inch grub with a slender profile and it should have a short, flat curly tail. Your retrieve should be slow and direct with an occasional drop. The slow retrieve will attract the bass, but it's the slow fall on the pause of the retrieve that will trigger the strike. This is the same retrieve I use when walleye fishing in spring with a jig and minnow.

Once the water temperature stabilizes into the mid-fifty degree range I continue to use a three inch grub but switch to one with a slightly fatter profile like a Kalin grub. However if a cold front moves in and the water temperature drops a few degrees I revert back to the slimmer profile grub.

The type of jighead you use is critical when fishing with grubs, especially in the cold water of spring. When fishing a clear water lake I leave the round head jigs in the tackle box and fish exclusively with darter head jigs. A darter head jig has a pointed head and a long shank with an oversized hook. As the name implies the darter head jig is designed for swimming applications and baits that are intended for moving along more rapidly. Almost exclusively poured on a 90 degree hook these jigs have their time and place, especially when searching flats for aggressive bass. The long hook shank allows the grub to sit horizontally and the oversized hook will maximize your hookset.

While fishing stained or slightly off colored water the darter head jig seems to have less of an advantage. The darter head is still best when fishing the flats but if bass are relating to rocks or holding on the edge of cover the round leadhead jig works fine. However when using a round leadhead jig make sure it has a quality hook. The color grub I choose when fishing clear water depends on the conditions. If it is a sunny day choose a translucent (somewhat clear, allowing light to pass through) colors with gold or silver flakes. When the sun passes through the grub the small flakes will have reflectivity that will mimic baitfish. My favorite grub colors are smoke, pumpkinseed and green pumpkin. On overcast days the reflectivity of the grub might actually turn the bass off. So stick with solid colors like black, motor oil, watermelon, and green pumpkin.

I did not use grubs in summer on these lakes since other presentations seemed to produce more fish. The only time when grubs would out produce all other presentations were when bass would suspend over open water. Just like in the strip mine that I fished in my younger days it would take some trial and error until you found the right jighead weight matched with the right grub. Only in the late summer period would I catch more suspended bass on a deep diving crankbait than a grub.

I do not fish clear lakes in the summer as often as I did in the past, since summer finds me on the river. If I am fishing a clear water lake for smallmouth or largemouth and I am hit with a summer cold front I will usually start and finish the day with a grub. That is not to say that my clients and I don't try other presentations it is just that the grub shines no matter how hard we try.

It was late July and my clients wanted to catch smallmouth from a lake. We had two great days on the river but one of my clients inquired about fishing smallmouth in a lake. I told them that the smallmouth action is more consistent on the river and that if we fished a lake we might not have very good success. Although my clients knew that the action would not be as good as it had been the last two days on the river, they wanted to learn how to fish clear water lakes for smallmouth in summer.

I picked them up in the morning and I told them we were going to fish a 1,000 acre lake that had a good smallmouth population with some huge smallmouth. On the way to the boat landing I told them that even though a minor cold front had passed overnight, we still had overcast skies which would work in our favor. I explained that the smallmouth would be either suspending over open water or structure, holding tight to cover or buried in the deep weeds. One of my clients asked what kind of lures we would be using and I quickly replied, "Grubs!"

After I launched the boat I told my clients that it would be trial and error until we found some smallmouth and developed a pattern. I told my clients that the first place we would be heading was a large point and I was looking for the smallmouth to be suspended off the deep edge of the point. I killed my outboard about one hundred yards short of the point and put down my electric trolling motor. I gave one client a 3/8 ounce darter head jig and a three inch black grub and the other client a 3/8 ounce darter head jig with a three inch watermelon red grub.

When we got about fifty yards off the point I stopped the boat and grabbed my rod with a 3/8 ounce darter head jig with a three inch green pumpkin grub. I suggested that my clients watch what I do since it is the perfect retrieve after a cold front. I made a long cast with the aid of my seven foot rod and four found test monofilament line, (this was in the days before fluorocarbon line). After the grub hit the water I let it sink for about ten seconds then jerked the rod tip causing the grub to dart rapidly and reeled in the grub with a slow steady retrieve. After I retrieved the grub about four cranks of the reel I repeated the jerking action. After I jerked the rod the third time and started my retrieve, I connected with a nice 17 inch smallmouth.

It did not take long for my clients to catch one and the first hour of fishing yielded six nice smallmouth from the deep edge of the point. After we landed the sixth smallmouth the action stopped and I told my clients that we had either caught all the active smallmouth that were suspending off the point or we had caught the only smallmouth suspending off the point. We continued to fish the entire point with grubs and a variety of crankbaits and plastics and could not stick one fish.

We proceeded to another point but the darting technique did not work. After casting several different baits it was obvious that nothing else would work either. Even though we were not catching any smallmouth my electronics showed several schools suspended at various levels; they definitely had lock-jaw. I told my clients that it was time to make another move and that this time we would see if we could snag a few smallmouth out of the weeds.

Our next spot was a deep weedline. I easily found the weedline but my electronics showed no fish. I explained to my clients that even though my electronics gave us the impression that no fish were present we were still going to fish the weedline and that grubs would remain the bait of choice. The big difference would be in the way that we would be presenting the grubs.

I stressed to my clients that after making a long cast parallel to the weedline, it would be important to let the grub fall to the bottom. After the grub fell to the bottom and they had slack in their line I told my clients to start a steady slow retrieve back to the boat. I positioned my boat so the two anglers could cast as parallel to the weedline as possible. I also stressed that we did not want to cast into the weeds but work the grub along the weed edge. Cold front smallmouth have a habit of holding just inside the weeds at the base of the weedline, and if the grub is too far from the base of the weeds a big smallmouth will not chase it.

John Pavlik with a weedline smallmouth

It took a while before one of my clients felt life on the end of the line but it was well worth the wait. The guy in the front of the boat commented that he could not tell if he was dragging the bottom or if he was getting light strikes. I told him that due to the cold front that he should not expect hard strikes and that he would need to concentrate and be patient. I added that we were using light line and medium light action rods so a soft hookset would work best. My client was surprised when the next light bite turned out to be a chunky 19 inch smallmouth. They caught several smallmouth by swimming grubs along the deep weedline and every smallmouth ended up pushing 18 inches or better.

Darter head grub jigheads that have the hook eye perpendicular to the hook shank will pick up weeds and on that particular day, I did not have an option. In recent years there have been many innovations in jighead design with several manufacturers designing jigheads with a narrow nose and the hook eye at the tip of the jig. This style of jighead will allow the grub to glide through weeds. These new jigheads make a grub even more deadly when fishing weeds.

Grubs catch both largemouth and smallmouth

After lunch we returned to the first point where we had all the early morning action. We tried darting the grub but had no success. I moved closer to the point and my electronics showed a big school of smallmouth suspending about a foot off the bottom. I told my clients to drop the jigs and let them hit bottom, tighten up the line and jig the jig a short hop. They repeated the procedure several times and eventually started catching smallmouth. I told them that if we were using round jigheads the grub would not be sitting horizontal in the water and the smallmouth would not be hitting the grubs. My clients were amazed at how they had caught smallmouth three different ways with the darter head and grub combination.

Grubs can hold their own with any artificial bait once the temperature starts to drop in the fall. Cold water should be approached differently in fall than in spring. In spring, bass activity will increase as water temperatures rise, while in fall, bass activity surges as the water temperatures drop. Spring bass tend to be scattered as they roam shoreline areas searching for food and warm water. By fall, they're ready to put on the feedbag and school up.

Fall fishing may sound easy, but you still need to determine the bite for the day, especially if you are searching for big bass. If you start with a large grub, you may get light strikes from big bass. Once a big bass hits, if he's not hooked, the odds of catching him are slim. If you are catching fish and they are hitting the grub hard, then try a larger grub, since the larger grub may result in larger fish. As the water temperature starts to rise during daylight hours, bass become more active, so the larger grub can become more productive especially if you are fishing in big fish water.

Smallmouth bass will suspend on many northern lakes in fall and a grub will allow the angler to vary his presentation until they make contact with a school of smallmouth. It is important that you keep a mental note as to how deep into the water column you are letting the grub drop before you start your retrieve. Knowing precisely how deep the smallmouth are holding is not that important, but it is critical that your grub gets into the strike zone.

I like to make a cast and count to five and start my retrieve. This will get me into the strike zone of smallmouth suspending high in the water column. I continue to let my grub fall with intervals of a five count, counting to five, ten, fifteen until contact, if any, is made. I have let my grub drop for as much as 30 seconds before making contact with smallmouth. When the grub gets to the desired depth, I will jig it a short hop and then start a steady retrieve back to the boat. Most of the time a 3/8 ounce or ½ ounce jighead with a four or five inch grub is the best combination.

Color can also be important and anglers should try to match the forage base as much as possible. If smallmouth are feeding on ciscoes or smelt use grubs that have blue, silver or white. Green pumpkin, pumpkinseed and motor oil might work in spring and summer, but I have not had good success with them when the smallmouth are feeding on ciscoes or smelt.

Grubs are not only effective in clear water lakes, they will also catch both numbers and big river smallmouth and largemouth bass. River smallmouth in particular will hit grubs from ice out through ice up. In fact I have caught a few river smallmouth over the years while jigging with small plastics for walleye.

A three inch grub is an ideal search bait for pre-spawn river smallmouth. I like to cast a three inch grub on a round leadhead jig along the edge of a river backwater. On the first few casts I will retrieve the grub on a ¼ ounce jighead just below the surface. This will trigger strikes from smallmouth cruising the edge of the backwater searching for baitfish. After I have sufficiently worked the top of the water column, I will use a heavier jighead with the same grub and let it drop while swimming the grub just off the bottom. My favorite spring grub colors when fishing rivers are chartreuse, white and watermelon red.

Any slack water shoreline area is good grub water. Cast the grub tight to the shoreline, let it drop and use a steady retrieve. You can hop the grub every now and then, but don't let it fall to the bottom. You will have a higher percentage of hook ups if you let the grub drop and then raise your rod tip and continue this retrieve. This technique also works well in reservoirs.

Summer smallmouth will cruise shallow rocks and for many anglers a grub is the bait of choice. When fishing small streams anglers like to use 2 or 2 ½ inch grubs on small jigheads. Personally I again chose a 3 inch grub but rig it on a 1/8, 1/16 or 1/32 ounce minnow head jig. Use the lightest possible jig that the depth and the current will allow. Even though the smallmouth are hunting crayfish on the bottom, they will still rise up to hit a grub. The minnow head jig will slide through the water and be less likely to get hung up in the rocks like a round head jighead. Since these shallow smallmouth are feeding on crayfish, watermelon red, pumpkinseed, and any grub with gold or copper flake will work best.

Another deadly grub tactic in shallow water is to buzz a twin tail grub on the surface. I will take a four inch curly tail and rig it weedless with a wide gap hook which will allow the grub to ride on the surface. When the grub hits the surface I give the grub a couple of fast hops and then burn the grub back to the boat. This technique works the best over mid-river grass beds where working a surface bait is tough. Big smallmouth can hold in open grass pockets and by the time your surface bait gets to the open pocket you are pulling a ton of grass on your sharp treble hooks.

In reservoirs grubs are also great when fishing rip rap, not only in summer but in spring and fall as well. When fishing rip rap with a grub, it is important to fish both perpendicular to the shoreline and parallel to the shoreline. When fishing perpendicular to the shoreline I will cast the grub tight to the shoreline and start my retrieve the instant the grub hits the water. After I retrieve the grub about three cranks of the reel I let it drop and dart it back to the boat just like when fishing a clear water lake. When fishing the grub parallel to the shoreline I will swim the grub back to the boat.

A grub is an excellent cold front bait in summer when nothing else seems to work. I have had many days when a three inch grub saved the day. When using a grub after a cold front, retrieve the grub as slowly as possible. My favorite technique is to let the grub fall about half way into the water column, raise up my rod about one foot and reel in just fast enough to keep the line taught. If the grub hits bottom, drag the grub along the bottom for about three cranks of the reel, raise your rod up one foot and then speed up back your retrieve back to the boat. Many times lifting the grub off the bottom will trigger a strike from a big smallmouth.

In early fall smallmouth can be in a transition and thus tough to locate. In this instance, with the exception of a crankbait a grub is the second best search bait. In fact, if you are fishing with a partner it is a good idea for one guy to fish a crankbait and another guy to fish a grub. Unlike a crankbait which will run at a certain depth, the grub will allow the angler to cover different depths and different types of cover. You can swim a grub over rocks, dart it along the bottom and vertical jig it between rocks making it a deadly bait in the hands of the right angler.

Big fall smallmouth that hit a grub

Just as in summer a fall cold front can slow down the river smallmouth bite even on a top smallmouth river like the Menominee River. With the exception of live minnows a three inch straight tail grub should be your go-to bait. Swim the three inch straight tail grub as slowly as possible but make sure you keep the grub off the bottom. When I feel even the slightest resistance I count to three and use a soft hookset. My favorite straight tailed grub colors are white and chartreuse.

Straight tail grubs will also catch big river smallmouth during all types of fall conditions. I use four inch grubs until the water temperature drops below 40 degrees when three inch grubs get the nod. Round leadhead jigs will work with straight tail grubs but darter head jigs will let the grub sit horizontally which will ultimately catch more smallmouth.

While it might not be considered a finesse presentation, every angler should have a few five inch grubs in their bag of tricks. Five inch grubs are primarily used for largemouth bass but on the Great Lakes anglers will use them to catch football sized smallmouth in the fall. Bass fishermen rig just about every soft-plastic Texas-style, but few bassers ever make a grub weedless. Nevertheless, a 5-inch grub rigged weedless and with a sliding bullet sinker is tough to beat when bass are holding tight to cover in cold water. During the cold water period, bass often move into very heavy cover and are not in a mood to chase baitfish let alone a lure. This type of habitat includes brushpiles, logjams and beaver huts; a 3-inch grub on a jighead is simply not going to pass through this type of cover. But a Texas-rigged 5-inch grub can nestle down into the thick stuff and be inched through it. The angler can also pause the grub, letting it sit motionless for long periods of time, move it a few inches and again let it sit. Sooner or later, a lethargic bass may well decide that a 5-inch grub offers size and bulk enough to make it worthwhile for the predator to move from its winter lair.

It is important to choose the right line and I prefer fluorocarbon line in clear water lakes and fluorocarbon/monofilament hybrid line when fishing grubs in rivers. These lines have limited stretch and will work in all situations and water temperatures. I like to avoid super lines since they are no-stretch line and anglers have a tendency to set the hook once they detect a strike. The problem is the fish will grab the tail of the grub and a quick hookset will result in a missed fish. Fluorocarbon line will allow for maximum depth penetration with the grub.

Monofilament line has a stretch that will work to your advantage when the bite is light. When the bass hits the grub, a slight stretch in the line will allow the bass to engulf the grub before the hook is set. Under a cold front condition, when the water temperature drops a few degrees, a bass can hit the grub, but it may take a few seconds before the angler detects the bite.

When choosing a rod for grub fishing you need to consider the size of the grub. For fishing three or four inch curly tail grubs or straight tail grubs a spinning rod will work best. I use a six foot six rod with a fast tip to detect the slightest strike, but plenty of power to get a hook set. If you use a rod that is too light, you will not be able to get a good hookset. Too stiff a rod, and you will not detect a slight pick-up. If I am fishing an extremely clear water lake under cold front conditions I will use a seven foot rod to enable me to make the longest possible cast. If you are fishing a five inch grub in heavy cover a bait-casting rod with more power is preferred.

While grubs excel in cold water, they will catch bass under almost any condition. Not only will you catch more bass consistently, but you'll get larger ones as well. If you are fishing heavily fished water, as many anglers do, you will be surprised at how effective grubs can be. Patience is the key to success – that and a nice fat grub!

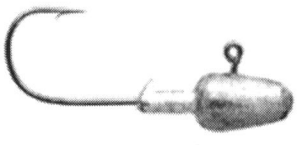
Darter head jig

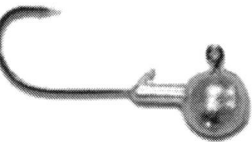
Ball head jig

Owner bullet head jig

Curly tail grub

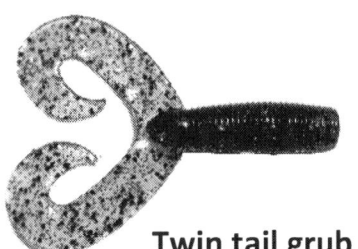
Twin tail grub

Straight tail grub

Chapter 3
Skirted Grubs

    Skirted grubs are also called Hula grubs or spider jigs and are made by a host of manufacturers. Three and four inch skirted grubs are the most popular with anglers. They come in both single-tail and twin-tail configurations. The skirt on the front of the grub body slows the jig's rate of fall and pulses enticingly in the water. The curly tail undulates when you pull it through the water. Most skirted grubs are impregnated with salt and are scented with garlic.

The original spider grub was developed by Bobby and Garry Garland around 1974 after they revolutionized the bass fishing world with the Gitzit tube. Initially the Garlands experimented with rigging a tube jig in reverse to appear bare behind with tentacles up front to better imitate a crawdad. The Garlands split the back of the tube into tentacles and added a floater worm as a trailer. Next, the worm tail was split in half making two legs that vibrated. Eventually the split tail worm led to Bobby Garland developing the twin tail grub to place in the back of the reconditioned tube. To make the combination complete Garland added the weedless jighead that he had been exposed to while fishing on Bull Shoals in February 1974.

Since its development there have been a few improvements to the skirted grub, mainly in its durability and the consistency of the plastic. The original skirted grubs on the market were in two pieces with the skirt being glued to the grub. For the most part the skirt would easily pull away from the grub when it was cast or pulled through cover and some would even fall apart when rigging the bait on a jighead. They did catch fish but this lack of durability made them unpopular with some anglers. Today the skirt and grub are molded in one process so durability is no problem.

I started using skirted grubs in the Northwoods back in the late 70's for largemouth bass. I only used them occasionally since by that time I was a staunch Gitzit (Tube) supporter. I had a few in my tackle box but on most days the thought of using one never crossed my mind. Although I had read about them extensively in fishing magazines the only time I would cast a skirted grub was on a day when bass refused everything else in my tackle box and by the time I got down to the skirted grub I did not have any confidence in anything. That was until I entered a local bass tournament on my home reservoir and was introduced to a new style of fishing.

It was not until I fished in a bass tournament in the early 1980's on my home reservoir that I gained a new respect for skirted grubs. For a few weeks prior to the tournament I was guiding on the reservoir for walleye and smallmouth bass. The walleye fishing had been good and I was hammering the smallmouth just about everywhere that we fished. Most of the smallmouth were caught on leeches but I also caught several nice fish on Gitzits (tubes). Since I caught my fair share of smallmouth with the Gitzit I was very confident that I was in good shape to win the tournament.

The reservoir has an excellent smallmouth bass population but they were tough to catch with artificial lures. With most of the other tournament anglers concentrating on largemouth bass I knew that I would have prime smallmouth water to myself. If my smallmouth pattern was to fail my partner had several haunts that held some big bucketmouths.

My first stop on the morning of the tournament was a shallow rock point that broke sharply to 30 feet of water. We were looking for smallmouth to be roaming the shallows feeding on either crayfish or minnows. My partner was twitching a shallow running crankbait and I was throwing a three inch pumpkinseed Gitzit. We worked the point for a considerable amount of time but could not catch one legal sized smallmouth.

I said to my partner, "I am certain there are big fish here but all they want is a leech."

My partner replied, "Before we move, let me try one more thing."

I watched as he took a four inch skirted grub out of his tackle box and rigged the grub on a black stand up jighead. On his first cast he had no better results than he had had with any other lure that we had tried. I was just starting to ponder our next fishing spot when my partner yelled, "Get the net."

I was quick to get the net and we soon put an 18 inch largemouth bass into the boat; just to say the least, I was impressed. We knew we had to stay on the point since there had to be more bass present. It took about a half dozen more casts, with my partner showing me how he was hopping the skirted grub, but before he could finish explaining his technique another good sized largemouth smacked the bait. We fished the point for another ten minutes but did not get another strike with either presentation.

Since we were in a tournament and not fishing for pure pleasure, it was easy for my partner to convince me to switch out objectives and suspend my smallmouth game plan. I knew that if we did not catch smallmouth off of the first point we fished, the odds were slim that they would be active elsewhere. My partner had fished the reservoir extensively for largemouth bass and I had no problem with him taking me to his honey hole.

We went for a long boat ride to the northern end of the flowage to a small rock point with ample wood cover. There was both submergent wood in the form of stumps and emergent wood in the form of downed trees. I had fished the spot before with my partner and knew it was also known by other anglers in the tournament. As we approached the spot there were no other anglers in sight and with a little luck maybe we were fishing virgin water.

Since it was my partner's boat he was in charge of the trolling motor and I knew I was in good hands. Actually, as a guide it feels good to have somebody else in control of the boat once in a while. My partner continued to use his skirted grub and on about the third cast he caught a legal largemouth bass. It did not take long for him to catch another legal bass and he suggested that I grab one of his skirted grubs; not that I am stubborn or anything, but I figured that if I was following him up I would be better off with a different bait. Finally, after he boated his third legal largemouth bass from the wood it was my turn.

After my partner had hopped the skirted grub over and around the stumps, I pitched my Gitzit tight to one of the deep stumps and let it fall, gave it a twitch and my line became tight. Hoping that I did not snag the stump, I set the hook and yelled at my partner to get the net. I knew the bass felt big, but was shocked when my partner scooped it into the net. We quickly measured the bass before putting the 21 inch hawg into the live well. We knew that if we could catch a few more bass we would probably win the tournament.

Unfortunately, we fished several spots the rest of the day and caught lots of bass but only one was a legal bass, it was also caught on a skirted grub. So we went into the weigh-in with 7 bass and had to settle for second place. However, the 21 inch largemouth weighed in just over six pounds which took the big fish pot. Any largemouth bass that pushes the six pound mark in the northwoods is a trophy.

The guys that won the tournament had their limit of ten bass. We had fished some of the same places that they had fished and it appeared that most of the largemouth they had caught came off rocks. After the weigh-in I did manage to get a bit of information off the record and one of the guys in the winning boat told me that they had caught most of them slowly retrieving skirted grubs. As far as I could tell they were using the same color that we were and a similar jighead.

That was my first experience with skirted grubs and it was interesting to say the least. Both the first and second place teams had caught most of their bass on skirted grubs, with one boat fishing rocks and the other concentrating on wood. The skirted grub had caught fish on two different types of structure by anglers using two different presentations. The $100,000 question was, would it be one of those "Hot Baits" that everyone had to have and then a few years later wither on the vine? Or would it be like the Gitzit, a bait that you could count on. Needless to say, ever since that day, I have been a firm believer in the skirted grub.

Many of my clients will ask me what the advantage or disadvantage of a skirted grub is when compared to a tube. That would depend on the time of year and type of cover you are fishing. But in general, while a skirted grub will catch both largemouth and smallmouth bass it is more suitable for largemouth bass. This is not to say that a skirted grub will not catch smallmouth, but most of the time a tube will out produce the skirted grub.

This comparison is especially true when fishing small clear water natural lakes. Most of these lakes have limited weed growth with structure often being at a premium. Some lakes have a mixed smallmouth and largemouth bass population while others will have just one dominant bass species. On lakes where smallmouth are present, tubes are hot and smallmouth will only rarely strike a skirted grub. On the other hand if largemouth bass are present they will prefer a skirted grub over a tube.

One of the strangest days I ever had on the water was in mid-July while fishing a 125 acre clear water lake. The small lake has a maximum depth of 30 feet, a few scattered deep weeds, two small islands, one rock pile and plenty of shoreline wood and boat docks. I told my client that the lake had both smallmouth and largemouth bass and that he could expect to catch both species, often in the same area. It was a typical July day with high humidity and no wind. The one factor in our favor was the over- cast skies.

My client loved to fish tubes so I told him to rig up a three inch watermelon red tube on a 1/8 ounce jighead. We were quickly on fish and while my client was reeling in his first 15 inch smallmouth he commented on the big school of smallmouth following the hooked smallmouth. Knowing my client could handle the smallmouth I quickly pitched a skirted grub into the school and readied myself to set the hook. The problem was that the strike never came.

After releasing the smallmouth my client made another cast with the tube and hooked another smallmouth. Again the school of smallmouth followed the hooked fish and again I flipped my skirted grub right in the midst of the big school. Needless to say I could not coax one smallmouth bass to take an interest in my skirted grub. While I was intently trying to catch a fish, my client dropped the tube into the school and immediately hooked another smallmouth.

Weedline smallmouth that hit a skirted grub

I was just ready to replace the skirted grub with a tube when I noticed a felled oak tree dropping into twenty feet of water. I knew there had to be bass there since the trees always held fish. I made a perfect cast and could feel my skirted grub which was rigged on a ¼ ounce stand up jighead hit a tree limb. After it slid off the tree limb I felt a "thump" and I set the hook into an 18 inch largemouth bass. As I reeled in the largemouth, I told my client to cast at the tree and within a few seconds he had a fish. However, instead of an 18 inch largemouth he had connected with a 17 inch smallmouth.

After we released both bass we both made casts at the twin oak trees and repeated the previous event. I caught a largemouth bass and my client caught a smallmouth bass. Kiddingly, my client commented that I could keep getting those largemouth out of the way so he could keep catching the smallmouth. I just smiled and made a cast at another tree and caught another largemouth bass. I was happy that my client was enjoying himself and as a bonus, I was also catching some fish. Many times while guiding I need to concentrate all my efforts to make sure the client is on fish and I don't get a chance to wet the line.

After that we fished a variety of different structure and depths and yielded the same results. It did not matter if we fished weeds, rocks or wood, my client caught smallmouth with the tube and I caught largemouth bass with the skirted grub. We even fished some deep sand grass which was the last place I would expect to find largemouth bass and we had the same results. I could have easily switched to a tube and caught smallmouth but I was determined to figure out how I could catch smallmouth with the skirted grub. I switched colors, changed jigheads, hopped the skirted grub and swam it across the bottom and not one smallmouth was interested in my offering.

We had an excellent day on the water with my client catching 42 smallmouth bass that day while I caught 23 largemouth bass. Anytime you put over 60 bass in the boat you can't complain. Although we did not catch any wall hangers we had plenty of action which is typical for a July day in the Northwoods. Besides catching all these bass we were the only bass anglers on the lake with the only other boat on the water holding a couple of people fishing for bluegills.

My client caught all the smallmouth bass on a tube and I caught all the largemouth bass on the skirted grub. Call it a fluke if you want, but I believe that this was a definite pattern. The only thing that was a factor is that the smallmouth were hitting the tube before it could fall into the cover where the largemouth were holding. It is common for smallmouth to suspend off the edge of cover and weeds and for largemouth to hold in the cover. Were the smallmouth avoiding the skirted grub and enabling it to drop into the wood, hence letting the skirted grub enter the largemouth bass strike zone? Or was the jig falling too rapidly to attract smallmouth. I can't answer that question but all I know is that on that day smallmouth hit the tube and largemouth hit the skirted grub. I have faced this scenario many times over my 30 years of guiding, but never to this extreme.

One deep clear water lake that I have fished regularly over the years has a dominate smallmouth bass population with a few token largemouth. The lake covers 1,000 acres with a maximum depth of 110 feet. Both ciscoes and rainbow smelt are present in the lake so both the smallmouth and largemouth bass grow to record proportions. Due to the clear water, with the exception of suspending jerkbaits and crankbaits if you did not use light line and finesse presentations you would not catch any bass.

The only real structure in the lake besides deep sand grass is fish cribs. There are several places where fish cribs are scattered along the shoreline in about 15-20 feet of water. They were put there years ago and in some cases are deteriorating. Even though they are far from in perfect shape, every time I fish the lake I find fish relating to these cribs. If I can't catch any bass off the fish cribs I might as well put the boat back on the trailer and head to a different lake.

Since I know the lake like the back of my hand I know which cribs would produce fish at specific times of the year and under certain weather conditions. This had more to do with the location of the fish cribs to spawning areas, available forage and their proximity to deep water. In spring, pre-spawn smallmouth and largemouth would stack up in cribs close to spawning areas and after spawning return to the comfort of the crib. Later in summer and fall cribs that were close to deep cover would hold more forage and attract more bass. On a few occasions I would find isolated fish cribs that never held fish due to their poor location.

Most of the time when I would fish the cribs on this lake my clients would catch a mixed bag of smallmouth and largemouth bass. The condition of the fish crib seems to dictate which species of bass was the primary predator. The more deteriorated cribs would hold a higher percentage of largemouth bass and the cribs that remained in good condition had a dominate smallmouth bass population. If a crib was in fair condition it would hold an equal amount of both largemouth and smallmouth bass. The condition of the fish crib and the species of bass it attracts seems to be a pattern on most northern lakes that I fish.

While both smallmouth and largemouth bass would relate to the fish cribs we needed to refine our presentation differently to catch each species. For smallmouth I will move in quietly with my electric trolling motor and cast a tube or curly tail grub 25 -30 yards away from the deep edge of the crib looking for suspended fish. After we catch the suspended smallmouth and even if we don't, I would move closer to the crib and grab my rod with a four inch skirted grub and a 1/4 or 3/8 ounce stand up jighead with a wire weed guard. The next step was to cast the skirted grub as tightly to the fish crib as possible, hoping to let the skirted grub bounce off the side of the fish crib several times and let it drop to the bottom. If we got a hit from a smallmouth it was when the skirted grub was falling. Most of the time the strikes occurred as the skirted grub bounced off one of the cribs' logs. Both twin tail and single tail skirted grubs work on smallmouth but I have caught more smallmouth with single tail skirted grubs. My largest smallmouth caught using this presentation was a real monster that measured 22 ½ inches.

Mike Gumila with a crib related largemouth

The presentation needed to catch largemouth bass was totally different since the largemouth bass would stack up in the inside of the fish crib. The inside of the fish crib was a conglomeration of logs, brush and rocks. Holding the boat on the deep side of the fish crib, I would cast to the inside of the inner edge of the crib and let the skirted grub rigged with a bullet sinker and a 3/0 wide gap hook hit the bottom. It was critical to keep as far away from the crib as possible being careful not to spook any fish. Once in a while a big largemouth would hit the skirted grub on the drop but these tended to be smaller bass. To avoid the strikes from the small bass, it is important to use a heavier bullet weight like a ½ ounce. The heavier bullet weight will drop quickly through the water column and also fall tight to the inside edge of the crib.

When you feel the grub hit bottom slowly tighten up the slack. Once your line is tight give the skirted grub a vigorous hop and let it drop back to the bottom and wait five seconds. Next, give the skirted grub another hop and drag it along the bottom about one foot. Continue this retrieve until you reach the opposite end of the crib. When you feel a strike set the hook hard and fast since largemouth will usually inhale the grub and you won't need to worry about light strikes. If you have patience a skirted grub will catch big largemouth bass from inside of the fish cribs. On some days we would catch largemouth bass from 50 percent of the cribs that we fished.

This pattern is almost a guarantee from spring through fall, not only on that particular lake but also on most lakes with fish cribs. As far as color goes for either bass specie, I stick with green pumpkin, watermelon and pumpkin pepper. I prefer a spinning reel since I seldom use any line heavier than six pound test while fishing clear water. I use either fluorocarbon line or fluorocarbon/monofilament hybrid line. When fishing cover inside the fish crib I use eight pound fluorocarbon line. Even though I am fishing in heavy cover, heavier line will cut down on the strikes. If given the option, I would rather lose a fish than get less strikes. A six foot six medium action rod with a fast tip works best. You might get a longer cast with a seven foot rod but I believe you get a better hookset with a six foot six rod.

Skirted grubs do not seem to be the ticket in current during the pre-spawn. Dragging or hopping a skirted grub off the bottom in cold water does not trigger strikes from non-aggressive fish. However, if you move a few miles downstream to the reservoir you have a different situation. Once the water temperature climbs above 50 degrees, a skirted grub is a deadly presentation. They seem to work best in staging areas as opposed to actual spawning sites. The best time to use a skirted grub is after a cold front.

I remember one particular May day when skirted grubs caught several smallmouth over five pounds for two of my clients. A few days prior to the cold front smallmouth were starting to stage in their spawning areas with the water temperature climbing to 56 degrees by early afternoon. I knew that this day would be tough since the cold front would push the smallmouth out of the staging areas and I might have a tough time trying to locate them. We fished the first break-line with tubes and wacky worms with little to show for our efforts. Casting crankbaits enabled my clients to boat a few small male smallmouth but they were scattered. Again, it was one of those days that can be a nightmare for a guide.

It finally dawned on me that maybe the smallmouth were holding in the stumps that were behind the boat. I had caught smallmouth in the stumps before and it was time to make a move. The other thought that entered my mind was that even if we did not catch smallmouth maybe there would be a few largemouth bass swimming in the stumps that would supply action for my clients. Fish were fish and a guide has to do what he can so the clients can have some fun. So I turned the boat around and headed for the stumps.

I gave one of my clients a single tail skirted grub rigged on a wide gap hook with a bullet weight and the other client a shallow running crankbait. I told the client that I chose a single tail grub due to the cold front. I added that if we were fishing this wood under stable weather and warming water temperatures I would have chosen a twin tailed skirted grub.

The client with the shallow running crankbait struck first before his partner had a chance to make a cast. He made a cast tight to a stump, twitched it and the water exploded. I hoped it was a big bass but I was dubious due to the size of the splash when the fish hit the bait. My client had either tied into a state record bass or a northern pike. Regrettably, my inclinations were right and once I saw the length of the fish and the tail, I knew it was no bass. It was a big northern pike and now the problem was to get the pike into the boat before the pike bit the line and ate my $10 crankbait!

Well, the pike won the battle and as my client reeled in his slack line he asked, "You got any more of those crankbaits."

Now, while I had a few more in my tackle box, I told him that was the last one and he gave me a funny look as I handed him a skirted grub. After all, I knew that if I gave the guy another crankbait he would cast it tight to another stump, twitch it, and probably hook another pike and loose another $10 crankbait. If he would have lost his crankbait and not mine I am sure he would not have tied on another one. Some clients just have no respect for the guide's tackle.

I told my clients to aim for the stumps, let the skirted grub fall and when they had slack line to give the grub a short hop and drag it slowly back to the boat. What I stressed most was the slow retrieve and that when they felt a strike to count to two before setting the hook. They made several casts without a pick up and the guy who lost the pike to a crankbait said, "I think we should be throwing crankbaits, they want a fast retrieve."

I was just getting ready to politely tell my client that we were after bass and not pike when his partner set the hook on what I thought was a big largemouth bass. This time I was glad it was not a largemouth bass as the fish turned out to be a 19 inch smallmouth bass. The smallmouth was a big pre-spawn female loaded with eggs and would have easily pushed 5 pounds. After my client took a few photos the smallmouth was released back into the water and headed right back to the stump. I was hoping that we had developed a pattern.

The water temperature started to rise and when it hit 54 degrees things started to happen. Mercifully, my client finally forgot about my crankbaits. The only problem he had was that his pattern was catching three smallmouth to his partner's one and his partner was also catching bigger ones. He was getting frustrated and was blaming himself. Needless to say by the end of the day skirted grubs caught 27 smallmouth with most of them being pulled out of the stumps and eight of them pushing the five pound mark.

While one of my clients was a better fisherman, it was obvious why he was catching more fish than his buddy. The guy who was catching most of the smallmouth had eight pound test Berkley XT line on his reel and the other guy was using some sort of braided line. When fishing for early season smallmouth in stained water after a cold front line is important. If we would have been fishing under better conditions there might not have been much of a difference in the number of smallmouth each client caught. However, after a cold front it is best to avoid braided line. When dealing with a cold front it is those little adjustments that will catch fish.

Skirted grubs will catch smallmouth in summer and I know many anglers who use them extensively in small rivers and streams. While I will occasionally cast a skirted grub over shallow rocks and weeds, I feel tubes, wacky worms and soft plastic jerkbaits are far more effective when fishing current on the mid-sized rivers that I fish. There have been a few occasions where skirted grubs have saved the day.

I have taken my fair share of big smallmouth while fishing deep rocks and ledges during summer. Keep in mind that when I am talking about deep water in the rivers that I fish I am referring to water under 12 feet deep. When river smallmouth are deeper than 12 feet they receive little attention since they are very tough to catch with artificial bait. I usually use a 3/8 or 1/2 ounce stand up or football head and cast it at a 45 degree angle up stream. Keeping my rod tip high I reel in the slack and use a fast retrieve making sure the jighead remains on the bottom. The trick is to keep the twin tails on the grub moving creating vibration. When I feel the bottom I give the grub an occasional hop. It can be difficult to keep the jighead on the bottom when retrieving in the current, and detecting a strike is not easy. With patience you can end up with a big smallmouth or two.

This same presentation is even more deadly in deep pools with limited current. If the pool has a combination of rock and wood they are magnets for big summer smallmouth. The lack of current allows the angler to feel the difference between the bottom and a strike. Since we are not dealing with current I prefer to make fan casts, trying to cover as much water as possible. If the bottom has a lot of wood take off the jighead and rig the grub weedless with a wide gap hook and a bullet sinker. Increase your retrieve speed, hop the grub erratically and hold on!

Skirted grub, football jig and a big river smallmouth

While skirted grubs might not be my first choice for catching river smallmouth in the fall they do have their place. They work best when smallmouth are holding off weed/rock transition areas. I like to cast the skirted grub tight to the weeds, let it drop and drag it onto the transition area. Once the grub enters the rocks, stop! Many times a big smallmouth will follow the grub along the weedline and hammer it on the pause. If you don't get a strike, start hopping the grub over the rocks and then swim it back to the boat. By using a different retrieve with different types of structure on the same retrieve you will increase your odds of triggering a strike.

For the most part crayfish imitation colors are in order when fishing rivers. Once the water temperature drops below 60 degrees I start to use both white and chartreuse skirted grubs. These colors are more distinguishable in stained water and resemble minnows. Since I am using a bait that resembles a minnow I will swim the skirted grub higher in the water column as opposed to dragging and hopping it along the bottom. On occasion I will rig up a white skirted grub and swim it about one foot off the bottom.

Although skirted grubs will catch largemouth bass at any time during the open water period they are most effective in spring and early summer in northern waters. On a natural lake once the water temperature reaches 55 degrees largemouth bass will move off the first breakline and hold on the edge of shallow bays. Later in the summer these same areas will have defined weedlines but in spring the weed growth is erratic. I will swim a skirted grub along the soft bottom around this scattered weedgrowth. In spring my preferred colors are watermelon, green pumpkin, pumpkin pepper and watermelon red.

When largemouth bass are scattered at different depths along a weedline a skirted grub can be effective. When rigging it on a stand up jig head you can both swim the grub at different depths and crawl it along the base of the weeds. It is important to first cover different depths along the weedline before working the base of the weeds. Top colors for fishing weedlines are green pumpkin, watermelon red and white. It is one of those baits that every bass angler should try when working a weedline.

skirted grubs catch reservoir smallmouth, they excel for early season reservoir largemouth bass. Just as with smallmouth they work best for pre-spawn fish as they move into staging areas. Largemouth bass will cruise the shallows and spend more time feeding prior to spawning than smallmouth bass. When they are cruising the shallows the forage that is at the top of the menu for a largemouth bass is a crayfish and any largemouth bass that is receptive to a crayfish will strike a skirted grub.

The most popular presentation in spring is for the angler to try to imitate a crayfish. Cast a four or five inch skirted grub tight to the shoreline and, as soon as it hits the bottom, start reeling it to give it a fast action until it hits bottom again. A roaming largemouth can come from a great distance to strike the bait that drops in the water. If the bait keeps moving an aggressive strike will occur. When the bait hits the water and stops, sometimes an aggressive bass will not strike the bait.

However, there are always a certain percentage of largemouth that are in the neutral mode and will require some coaxing. So when your first retrieve does not work, on the next cast let the grub hit bottom and try a series of hops, dragging the bait a few feet and then stopping. Then repeat the hop and drag retrieve back to the boat.

No matter what type of retrieve you are using it is important to keep contact with your bait and to keep slack line at a minimum. It is difficult to fish this presentation on a windy day since the wind causes your line to develop a bow causing you to miss strikes. When faced with a windy day one solution is to make shorter casts and to increase the weight of your jighead. If wind is a major problem don't hesitate to find areas out of the wind since they can hold more aggressive bass.

For largemouth bass I use a six foot six medium or six foot six medium/heavy action rod. Reservoir largemouth do not seem to be as line shy as smallmouth bass so you can use braided line if you desire. Some anglers like to use braided line due to the increased sensitivity. However, I personally prefer a spinning reel spooled with fluorocarbon/monofilament Hybrid line due to its limited stretch and good sensitivity. Monofilament line will also work.

Skirted grubs are also a great bait when largemouth bass are relating to rip rap shorelines, points and bridges. Make sure you adjust the weight of the jighead to the depth of the water you are fishing. A skirted grub can be fished in deeper water but other baits are generally more effective.

In general, the colder the water the slower the presentation needs to be. You should employ variations in your retrieve and try to remember what you were doing with the bait when you felt a strike. The more attention you pay to your surroundings the more fish you will catch. Remember skirted grubs might not catch the most fish but they catch a higher percentage of larger fish than other plastics.

Fall largemouth that engulfed a skirted grub

Skirted grub with weedless football jighead

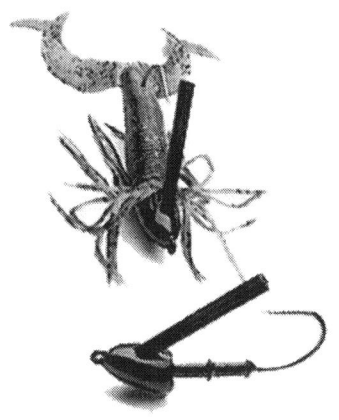

Skirted grub with a weedless bullet head

Chompers twin tail Skirted grub

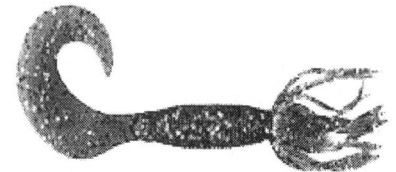

Yamamoto single tail Hula Grub

Football jighead

Yamamoto Hula Grub, and 3/0 wide gap hook

Chapter 4
Tubes

    Back when Bobby and Gary Garland worked together to design new plastic baits they had little idea how influential there designs would be. One lure in particular, the Gitzit, is still winning tournaments and can be found on the shelves of every tackle shop across North America.

    The Garland brothers invented the Gitzit (tube) which was the first hollow plastic bait. To fish the tube they inserted a light jighead into the hollow cavity of the bait. The story goes that they invented this bait to fish the shoreline moss beds on the Colorado River reservoirs. The idea was to cast this light bait on top of the moss without sinking into the moss. Then they would pull it off the moss and it would spiral down the moss edge on a slow fall to the bass. The idea worked and they began winning many tournaments with the Gitzit.

The little lure remained a secret of Western anglers until Bobby Garland was paired with Missouri angler Guido Hibdon in a tournament on Lake Mead. Hibdon quickly learned about the magic little 2.5 inch tub called the Fat Gitzit. He could not wait to take his new-found bait back east. Back east, anglers joked about the small lure, to them it wasn't a "finesse" lure it was a "sissy" lure. But, when Hibdon, won a few tournaments, the "sissy" lure started looking pretty tough. The rest is History!

The Gitzit and many other brands of tube baits are made of a rubbery plastic which is often firmer and more rubber like than other soft plastic baits. Usually, a tube bait is dipped and formed around a metal mandrel or rod. Then the tentacle-like tails are machine-split (sometimes not so neatly) as a later step in the process after the rubber cures or hardens. A very few brands of tubes are injection molded from the same soft plastics as most other soft baits and the tentacle tails are injected during the process, rather than split as a later step in the process. The injected tentacles are much neater, and although still not always perfect, they have a more fluid action in the water than the machine-split rubbery tails.

Even with all the new innovations in soft plastic baits, the tube remains unique. The hollowness of the tube makes it different from all other soft plastics. I believe that the hollow core gives the tube some of its life-like qualities. Even when the tube sits on the bottom and the angler does "nothing" current and wave action can make the tube pulsate making it irresistible to a bass.

Another important aspect of the tube is its uncut body length proportioned to the tail in order to create good hydrodynamic action of the tube. Just like the body and tail of a kite both balance to produce its best aerodynamic properties. A good length ratio of about 60% uncut body portion relative to 40% split tail portion. The length ratio of the uncut body portion helps to create the desirable wavering, zigzagging, side-to-side waffling or spiraling action absent in other plastics.

A high quality tube will include fine cut tails which result in quivering tentacles. The softness and separateness of the tube tails creates life-like vibration as each individual tentacle moves in the water. When a tube has many finely cut tentacles, there is an increased surface area of the bait exposed in the water causing additional drag. The tube is just as much of a sound bait as a sight bait.

Original Gitzit (tube)

A tube is probably the most versatile of all plastic baits, with tubes catching bass from the surface to the bottom in shallow and deep water throughout. Tubes are also effective bass catching baits during the entire open water period. Tubes can be fished around all types of cover due to their unlimited rigging options. They are one of the only baits that I have enabled me to catch bass regardless of the weather pattern. Form stable weather patterns to the most adverse cold front, if you can't hook a bass on a tube I doubt any other bait will work.

Being a smallmouth aficionado, most of my experience with tubes has been in pursuit of these denizens. Most of the time, I will use a 3-inch or smaller tube on light or medium light action spinning tackle. When rigging a tube for smallmouth I find myself using the basic method of inserting a jighead into the hollow body of the tube. This finesse presentation will work both on clear water natural lakes and stained water reservoirs and rivers.

Rigging a tube with a jighead will allow the angler to catch smallmouth regardless of their mood. However, the action of the tube can be affected by the position of the jig head inside the tube body. With the head pushed all the way forward, tubes tend to fall faster with less spiral, which is great for active smallmouth. When smallmouth are less-aggressive, slow down the fall of the tube and increase the spiral, by positioning the jig head back from the nose of the tube. Changing the way the tube is rigged on the same jighead can turn a slow day into a banner outing. There have been many occasions when what seemed like a slight modification resulted in a change in the bite. On a few rare occasions a radical change yielded outstanding results.

On a few memorable occasions having a client with limited fishing knowledge has led to my client catching a few more fish than the guide. One summer day in the early 1990's I had a client fishing with me who along with having limited fishing knowledge had never fished with a tube before. I assured him that fishing a tube was not rocket science and that by mid-day he would be catching bass like a pro. What I did not expect was my client to show the guide a new way to fish a tube.

We started fishing a rocky shoreline looking for smallmouth to be foraging on crayfish. It took a while but eventually my client caught his first smallmouth bass on a tube. I grabbed the fish and after I released it into the water I inspected the tube and told my client that it was critical that he check the tube after catching a fish to ensure it was rigged properly.

My client caught a few more fish and I also got into the action. However, the action came to an abrupt halt. We must have fished for at least 45 minutes without a strike. I switched to a grub and after observing my clients' ragged tube I told him that it was time for a fresh tube.

I reached into my bag of tricks and pulled out a fresh tube and told my client to pass me his rod. My client said, "No need for that, I can rig up my own tube". I thought, "No problem," tossed him the tube and made a cast with my grub. I had no response with my grub and was ready to change baits when my client yelled, "Got one!"

Not only did he have a smallmouth, but it was by far the largest fish of the morning. As I slid the net under the 19 incher I noticed that something about the tube looked funny. As I grabbed the fish I noticed that the tube was reversed on the jighead. My client had placed the hook of the jighead through the nose of the tube with the eye of the jig protruding through the tentacles.

I was dumbfounded! How do you tell a client who just caught the largest fish of the morning that he rigged the tube the wrong way? I suppose that some guides would have demeaned the client and told them they just got lucky, but being an inquisitive angler, I thought to myself, let's try this again. Was it just a freak or was this greenhorn on to something. So for the moment I said nothing, hoping my client would repeat the procedure and catch another bass.

It was hard for me to watch my client without making him feel on edge with me staring at him. I was trying to monitor his expert presentation so if need be I could duplicate it. If my client had caught a 15 inch smallmouth it would not have been a big deal, but when someone catches a 19 incher, you try to figure out if it was a fluke or a definite pattern. Just as I was convincing myself that it was a fluke, my client ripped into another big smallmouth.

After I released my clients' second big smallmouth, I figured it was time to tell him that his method of rigging tubes was contrary to mine. I asked him if there was a reason for his method and he said, "No, I just figured that it didn't matter how it was hooked."

I explained that the way that the tube is rigged is critical to the tubes' action. I also mentioned that there is no right or wrong way to rig the tube. After my client made another cast, I also used his unique presentation. It worked the rest of the day and we ended up catching at least 12 smallmouth over 18 inches on the backward tube rig. Since that day I never say no to a client that asks if they can concoct a new way to rig a tube.

In general, for smallmouth bass I use two basic presentations; either hop and reel or dragging the tube. Both methods have their place and can shine on any given day. The hop and reel method is probably the most popular and the easiest to perfect.

Having spent a considerable amount of time jigging for walleyes it was an easy transformation for me when I began hopping a tube. All you need to do is make a cast and reel up the slack in your line until it becomes taut like you would with a jig and minnow. Then lift the rod and make a few twitches with the rod tip sending your jig upwards a few inches or a foot, then allowing it to come to rest once again on bottom. Continue with this rhythm until you have worked the tube back to the boat or you catch a fish.

A smallmouth will do one of two things during this retrieve - bust your bait while it is spiraling on slack line, or suck it up while it is motionless on the pause. Pay close attention to your line for any movement as this will signify a hit from a fish. Smallmouth can suck up a jig and spit it out in the blink of an eye, so concentration and visualizing what is happening below the surface is crucial.

Dragging a tube across humps, rocks, or the river bottom can be a very deadly presentation, since it imitates the movement of a crayfish. When an angler drags a tube, he should also know the habits of the crayfish. For the most part, crayfish will crawl horizontally along the bottom. If you have ever watched crayfish move along the bottom they will exhibit sudden bursts of speed but for the most part they are lethargic as they move along the bottom. A bass will monitor the crayfish movements and go in for the kill when it pauses.

When I drag a tube, I am in the mindset that there is a live crayfish on the end of my line. The only thing that I do differently than most anglers is I don't let the tube sit motionless on the bottom. After I pause the tube, I slowly reel in the slack, and when the line is taught, I raise the rod tip a few inches and slowly drop it back down. What this does is cause the tentacles of the tube to quiver which resembles the legs of the crayfish. A smallmouth cruising the rocks will find the tube irresistible. Even though most tubes on the market are heavily salted and scented, it never hurts to add a little added scent to your tube. The scent won't attract the smallmouth but it can cause the bass to hang on to the tube longer and increase your rate of hook sets.

Two smallmouth caught while dragging a tube

While it is not difficult to learn, many anglers don't have enough patience to fish a tube properly under all conditions. If the smallmouth are aggressive, there is no need to quiver the tube on the lake or river bottom. But if the bite is light the ability to coax a wary smallmouth will work to your advantage.

Dragging a tube in deep water can be especially productive when river smallmouth are holding in the main river channel. While it is a deadly tactic under a stable weather pattern it is especially productive after a summer cold front. Summer cold fronts usually have a minimal effect on river smallmouth but there is a definite slow-down in the bite. While a big smallmouth holding tight to the bottom might not be eager to rise up to strike a bait, it can find a scented tube placed right in front of its nose irresistible.

Pre-spawn smallmouth can be very susceptible to any weather change; even a slight change in wind direction or change in light penetration can change the bite. The worst case scenario during the pre-spawn is a cold rain that moves in after you have developed a pattern and are sticking fish. The cold rain will drop the water temp. a degree or two and push smallmouth tight to the bottom. While they might not move to deep water, they will hold tight to cover and won't chase a bait.

One early May day the sun was shining, the water temperature was a balmy 60 degrees and smallmouth were in the late stages of the pre-spawn. We were catching smallmouth with soft plastic stick baits and I suggested that one of my clients tie on a surface bait. On the third cast my client boated a 20 inch smallmouth and I quickly handed my other client a similar topwater bait. The topwater action was really starting to heat up along with the water temperature and everything was pointing to an excellent day on the water.

 Everything looked great except for the rumble of thunder and the black sky off to northwest. At first I did not pay it any mind since the weather forecast was for a chance of a spotty shower late in the afternoon. I was only 11 am so according to the weather man we had several hours before we had any chance of rain. After all, the weather man is never wrong.

Well, as you might have guessed, it did not take long for the rain to set in. It was a cold spring rain and needless to say the topwater bite came to an abrupt halt. I have been there many times before and I knew that we could put the topwater baits back in the box. I also knew that the only way we were going to catch smallmouth under these conditions with the exception of live bait was to drag tubes. I dug through my bag of tricks and gave one of my clients a watermelon red tube and the other a pumpkin pepper tube rigged on a 1/8 ounce tube jighead.

Pre-spawn , cold front smallmouth

After I convinced my clients that the only way they were going to catch smallmouth was to drag the tube slowly along the bottom and use a few short hops they began to connect with fish. It was not a banner day, and while the bite was light my clients managed to catch smallmouth the rest of the day. The fish we caught might not have been 20 inchers, but it was action none the less. Tubes saved the day again!

On natural lakes and reservoirs, rocky mid lake humps are prime holding areas for summer smallmouth bass. Under stable weather patterns the active smallmouth can usually be found suspended off the edges of the hump. If smallmouth are not suspending on top or off the edges of the hump feeding on baitfish, they are probably holding tight to the bottom feeding on crayfish. When they are feeding on crayfish, dragging a tube over the hump is the ticket. It is important to work the entire hump and the deeper edges. Experience has taught me that the largest smallmouth will relate to the deep edges after a cold front.

After a summer cold front, the only bait that will out fish a tube for these bottom hugging smallmouth is a live jumbo leech. While I am guiding I will often use both tubes and leeches since most of the time a leech is a no brainer. I attach a split shot about 16 inches up from the leech which is rigged on a number four live bait hook. All the angler has to do is drop the leech down to the bottom and occasionally jig it off the bottom a few inches.

Using a tube will require a bit of concentration and the average angler will miss more fish than they catch. I use the same rod and line when using both the tube and leech. A six foot six or seven foot medium light action rod with my reel spooled with either a six pound fluorocarbon/monofilament hybrid or fluorocarbon line. What usually happens is that after my client catches a few smallmouth on leeches, if I feel they have enough dexterity to finesse a tube I show them my unique technique.

First, I make a long cast which will enable me to cover as much area as possible with my tube. After the tube hits the bottom, reel in the slack and give the tube a few vigorous shakes. Next reel in the slack and watch the line for any movement. If you see the lightest line movement, tighten up the line and set the hook. Next on the agenda is to slowly retrieve the tube about two feet, and again vigorously shake the tube. The trick is to not stop the tube but to combine the slow steady retrieve with the shaking of the tube. Most of the strikes will occur just as you stop shaking and start retrieving the tube.

I believe that this will get the attention of smallmouth within visual distance of the tube to hit it. Just as a live squirming leech will out produce a docile nightcrawler, a slowly crawled and shaken tube will induce more strikes. If you stop the retrieve on a hump, smallmouth tend to be less likely to hit the tube than when they relate to other types of structure. This is a big fish tactic! Honestly, I don't know why, but what I do know is that this technique has boated many a 20 inch plus smallmouth over the years. It works best in clear water due to the increased visibility. In the past I have used monofilament line but in recent years fluorocarbon line has only enhanced this presentation.

Nose hooking a tube can be deadly when fishing shallow water. I found this out on an early May guide trip when the conditions were more in line with mid-July. As we hit the water the conditions were perfect: light southwest winds, clear skies and water temperatures in the low sixties. I told my client that I had never seen water temperatures this warm so early in the season. I also added that if the water warms too quickly pre-spawn smallmouth can be confused and fishing can be tough to pattern.

Confused they were, since we fished several shoreline points and rocky shorelines with only a few small male fish to show for our efforts. Although these male smallmouth were aggressive and easy to catch, we were hoping to connect with larger smallmouth, since we were fishing during the pre-spawn. We fished for about an hour with no better results. Next, I moved to a small rock which rises in the middle of a shallow bay. This was a spot where I catch lots of 12-15 inch smallmouth early in the season. I had almost given up on catching big smallmouth and decided that we would concentrate on numbers.

I told my client that we would be fishing in extremely shallow water and that instead of rigging a tube on a jighead or Texas style with a worm weight, we would be using my modified live bait tube rig. This is the same rig that I use when fishing a leech or nightcrawler in shallow water, nothing more than a split shot and a hook. I tie on a number two or number four octopus or live bait hook and nose hook the tube. Next I clinch a BB sized slit shot up about 16 inches from the hook. If there is no wind I will eliminate the split shot. My choice in tube is again the original Gitzit style.

I explained to my client to cast out the tube and do nothing with it for about ten seconds, then slowly reel up the slack and watch his line. You need to be observant and watch your line as the smallmouth will suck in the tube and slowly move it away. In extremely shallow water, if a smallmouth feels any weight as they move the tube they can drop it. When you detect a strike make sure you feel the weight of the fish before you set the hook. If you fail to detect a strike or line movement, raise the rod tip, slowly reel in the slack and again watch the line.

Nose hooked tubes catch big shallow water smallmouth

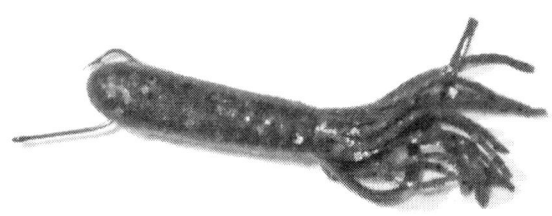

Nose hooked tube

My client rigged up a watermelon red tube, made a cast towards the rock and in a few seconds he reeled in a chunky 19 inch smallmouth. We continued to catch several smallmouth on tubes and all of them were loaded with crayfish. Since we were fishing in less than one foot of water, a jighead would have resulted in snags. Had the tube been rigged with a worm weight, the smallmouth would have felt resistance.

On a few occasions when fishing extremely snag infested water I will place a piece of Styrofoam inside the tube. I will place the small BB split shot up about one foot. This will allow the buoyant tube to float up off the bottom making the tube more visible from a distance. The more visible the tube is the more strikes that will occur.

What was happening was the water had warmed up so quickly that crayfish were all over this shallow rock looking for a meal. The water temperature by this time was 65 degrees, but smallmouth had put spawning on the back burner. Interestingly, we fished other similar rocky structure and could not catch a fish. These are just things that happen.

Since I started to rig soft plastic stick baits wacky style in the late 1990's I have at one time or another tried this rigging technique on most soft plastics. Some have worked while others haven't. You can put tubes into the good column. Wacky worming a tube will occasionally work around wood cover but rigging it Texas style is a more effective presentation. However, when the smallmouth are on their beds it is a very deadly tactic. I will use a 1/16 ounce or 1/8 ounce weedless wacky jighead, the same jighead you would use with a soft plastic stick bait.

By using the wacky style jighead the tube will have the horizontal drop of the stick bait but the hollow body will cause the smallmouth to suck in the tube instead of pushing it away from the nest. This can often be a problem with a soft plastic stick bait during the spawn. The only problem is the jigheads are very expensive, costing as much as a buck and a quarter apiece! That is perhaps why most of my customers have never seen me use this method. After all, when fishing in rocks, my clients could go through dozens by noon, especially when they are not paying for them. This is definitely a technique for the advanced angler. Fluorocarbon line works best for these early spawning smallmouth.

In summer I have also had good success wacky rigging a tube and letting it drift weightless over mid-river rocks and grass. The tube will float or sink only inches below the surface and on some days smallmouth will eat them like popcorn. Since I am not using an expensive jighead and snags are minimal even in mega rocky areas, it is an easy technique for even an inexperienced angler but one that seasoned bassers should also add to their arsenal.

What I do is cast the tube upstream over rocks and grass, let the tube drift downstream and, while keeping a tight line, twitch the tube and let it fall. To give the tube a bit of weight I will add a tiny BB sized split shot just above the eye of the hook. As far as a hook goes you can use either an octopus hook or a Kahle hook. This method has worked on days when smallmouth for whatever the reason were hitting the soft plastic stick baits lightly and my clients were having trouble setting the hook. It also works very well with overzealous kids.

For largemouth bass the most common rigging method is the Texas rig which will enable the angler to fish the tube around brush, trees, stumps, rocks, and vegetation. Another method is to Tex-pose the hook when fishing sparse cover, especially where the water is mostly open, with few snags or weed patches. Put the point into the bottom of the bait and all the way out the top of the bait. Tubes can also be rigged weightless for fishing at or near the surface. They can also be used with Carolina Rigs and drop shot rigs which will be covered in later chapters.

Largemouth bass like to hold under cover to escape sun and predators with typical holding areas including docks, boat houses, pontoon boats, and overhanging branches. For many, flipping and pitching is the preferred method to fish these kinds of cover. This enables the tube to be fished both tight to the edges and in the cover.

Flipping a tube is a modification of flipping a jig although they are both contact lures. The difference between the two baits is that the jig falls straight to the bottom whereas the tube falls more erratically. When you pop it off the bottom, the tube will also dart unpredictably from side to side as it settles back to the bottom.

Largemouth caught flipping a tube

When fishing heavy cover use the traditional Texas rig. Put the hook in through the bottom of the bait and have the point sitting just under and ready to come out the top surface of the tube. Sometimes, you can push the point out the top, then pull it back underneath. Never pull the entire barb out, then try to cover it back up with the plastic. If you pull the entire barb out, you will have made the channel too wide, and the hook point will poke out too easily and get stuck when you pull the tube over snags.

A Flippin' Tube, is a bit bigger and heavier than typical tubes, and therefore works best with a 3/0 or 4/0 hook. Most anglers use worm weights and 17 to 25 pound test mono with a seven foot six flipping sticks.

When using a tube for flipping, it is important not to stretch the tube too tightly onto the hook since this can make for poor hooksetting. A properly rigged tube will leave a slight amount of slack in the body between the offset eye and the embedded hook point. Leaving slack does not mean that the lure should look like it has a bend or curve caused by the way you rigged it, it should look perfectly straight. But when you press down on it with your index finger right where you want the fish to bite it, there should be some give in the tube. It is also important that the front portion of the hook eye is not jammed tight against the weight. Once the hook point starts to grab hold in the fish's mouth, you really want the entire tube to easily pull down off the front offset portion of the hook, and out of the way where it won't interfere with a good hookset. Flipping a tube will take time to master.

Pitching a tube is deadly when fishing thick weeds and on hot summer days when bass crawl under lily pads. The trick is to pitch the tube and let it fall quickly through the weeds and keep just enough tension on the line to feel the tube falling, while trying not to slow the fall as it slips through the cover. When it hits the bottom let it sit for two or three seconds, then shake it a few times before before picking it up and pitching again. Like a jig, the strikes generally occur on the initial fall or shortly after the bait hits the bottom. There are times when you will need to shake a tube in heavy cover for several seconds to "call" the bass to the bait. For the most part, pitching a tube is a technique used for covering water, so don't waste too much time working the tube on the bottom.

When pitching, most anglers will rig the tube with the traditional Texas rig. Tex-posing the hook is very popular with anglers who use rigged tubes. When Tex-posing the hook you leave the point of the hook exposed above the main body of the tube and placed either in the ribs of the tube or just laying it flat against the top of the bait. You can Tex-pose a hook on tubes without ribs by putting the point as close to the body as possible or by putting it slightly back into the skin of the tube.

There are times when a low trajectory and the small angle art of "skipping" a tube will give the angler an advantage. For example, picture yourself at a long dock with boats on either side. If flipping, you'd be limited to how much of the dock you could fish and you'd likely only be able fish the edges. By skipping a tube you will be able to thoroughly fish the area by bouncing the tube under the docks and boats. You will also be able to skip the tube through any open areas.

Skipping takes practice but when done properly, it causes a minimal splash and you will be able to cast baits a considerable distance. This makes it a great option in clear and shallow water. Bass appear attracted to the skipped tube as it mimics baitfish scurrying across the water, unlike hopping or dragging a tube which imitates a crayfish.

The rounded sleek profile of a tube will glide easily across the surface. To keep the tube snag resistant you need to rig them Tex-Posed using a 2/0 or 3/0 wide gap hook, matching the size of the hook with the tube body. Skipping is an aggressive presentation, so it is important to use a tube with a thick wall and a tough nose, to hold the hook in place.

You will need to add weight to tubes to cast them with enough force so they skip and then sink upon entry. You can either use weighted hooks or insert a weight into the tube. There are weights specifically designed for tubes but 1/16 to 1/4 ounce worm weights will also work. If you use a worm weight you will need to peg the weight with a tooth pick behind the weight. The weights' location on the tube will dictate the action of the tube. A front-weighted tube will nose dive in a tight spiral, while a center-weighted tube will shimmy or glide in a larger circle in a horizontal position.

Spinning gear works best for skipping. A spinning reels' stationary spool lets line unravel without tangles from the irregular surge-and-bounce pull of the line from a skipping tube. Most anglers use either 12 to 17 pound test fluorocarbon or 20 to 30 pound test superlines for their strength and abrasion resistance. Fluorocarbon is the best choice when fishing clear water.

When it comes to rod, short is the name of the game. While there are rods specifically designed for skipping tubes, I use a six foot rod that has a fast tip. This rod unloads quickly with the snap of my wrist but still has enough backbone to pull a bass out of cover.

Now for a lesson in the fine art of skipping a tube: Start with six to 12 inches of line between your rod tip and the bait. Use a side arm cast with the rod pointed slightly downward, keeping both hands on the rod to improve casting accuracy and control. With a quick turn of the wrist, spin the tube on the line so that it rotates around the rod tip in a clockwise motion. This will add momentum to the tube.

Immediately after starting to spin the tube, pull back on the rod and begin a side arm cast. As the tube completes half a rotation, snap the rod tip forward. In a perfect world the rod tip should unload as the tube completes 3/4ths of the rotation. At that point the tube should shoot forward at a low angle along the water. If the angle is too high, the tube will likely sink, make a big splash or bounce on too high of an arc to bounce again. If you have trouble in keeping the tube low to the water try crouching.

When trying to fish overhanging shoreline branches, you will need to have a slightly higher skipping angle. Aim the tube in front of the branches so that it breaks through the leaves after the first bounce. To get a higher bounce, either raise the rod tip slightly so the bait hits the water at a higher angle, or keep the bait low but add a stronger snap to your cast so that the tube skips high off the water.

Skipping is not as difficult as it sounds, but it will require lots of practice although some anglers catch on quicker than others. It will enable you to catch more bass from heavily fished waters. However, its biggest drawback is that it is only effective when the water is calm or has a slight ripple.

While tubes are great for largemouth bass many smallmouth anglers consider them to be the most important bait in their tackle box, and rightly so!

Tube rigged with a jighead

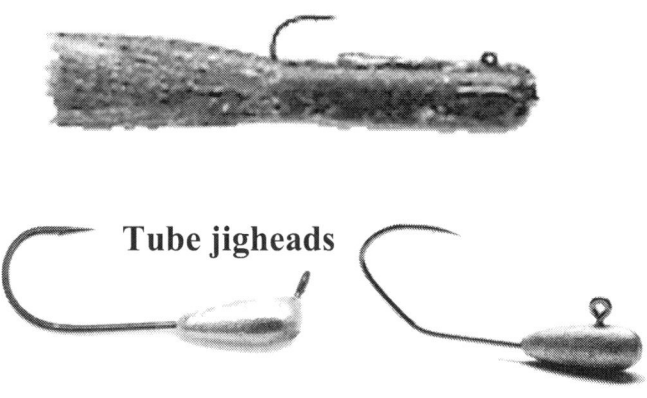

Texas rigged tube with inserted rattle

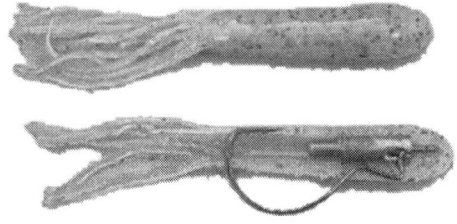

Flipping tube with weedless bullet head

Chapter 5
Wacky Worms & Stickbaits

    I first started to use finesse worms as a supplement to live bait. My clients didn't mind using live bait if they were catching fish but there is a bit more satisfaction if the angler thinks he is fooling the fish as opposed to feeding it. As you are finding out in this book I spend most of my non-guiding time on the water searching for new ways to catch bass.

    In the early 1990's I was determined to find a way to use plastic worms to catch shallow water smallmouth bass. Most plastic worms on the market were much too bulky for finicky spring smallmouth bass. I would get plenty of strikes but I had trouble setting the hook. I would switch to a grub and start catching fish, but again I was determined to catch them on a plastic worm. Four inch plastic worms rigged on a slider head were effective but I was constantly irritated by snags.

Sometimes a little common sense helps. Finally it hit me, why not rig up one of a four inch slider worm the same way that I rigged a live leech? It was simple, all I had to do was take a black worm, since it resembled a leech, tie on a number four live bait hook, (this was before they made octopus hooks), and place the hook through the head of the worm. Next, I clinched on a small split shot about 12 inches from the hook and I was ready to go.

I positioned the boat within casting distance of a small rocky island where I was confident a few big smallmouth would be cruising the shoreline. On my first cast I used the same presentation that I would be using if I was using a leech. After the worm hit the water I did nothing, letting the worm fall amongst the rocks. Before I had a chance to reel up my slack my line started heading for deep water. I quickly reeled in the slack and set the hook. The smallmouth looked like a female that had recently completed spawning.

This seemed too simple. Heaven only knows know why I didn't try this rig before. Well, since that time my practice of pitching a small finesse worm tight to shoreline rocks has caught many smallmouth, both for my clients and me. If there was not too much wind, I would rig up the worms without a split shot and if the conditions were right my clients would catch a boat load of fish. The only problem was that if there was any wind, you needed to add weight, and that usually resulted in a snag, especially if my client had limited fishing experience. I thought I had the ultimate technique until I decided to rig the worm a bit differently.

The other problem I faced was that with the worm hooked through the head the worm usually ended up on the shoreline if my client made too hard of a cast. On one particular day my client threw about a dozen worms into the woods and I was about ready to put a jumbo leech on his hook! Suddenly, out of rage I rigged up another worm and hooked it through the center. About that time I didn't care if my client caught any fish, I was just looking for a way to keep the worm on the hook.

Well, hooking the worm through the middle kept the worm on the hook alright but little did I know that it would catch smallmouth. In fact, my client caught 15 smallmouth after he hooked the worm in the middle, while all he caught was trees when the worm was hooked through the head. It is funny how some of the most effective ways to catch fish were developed by accident. While I am not claiming to have invented the wacky worm technique, I am just saying that I center hooked a finesse worm to accommodate my clients long before I ever heard of the term "Wacky worm."

I only used the center hooked finesse worm when fishing spring smallmouth in lakes and reservoirs. After smallmouth moved away from the shallows the light worm with no weight was not very effective. I tried it while fishing in shallow rocks in the river but the current kept the worm flowing too fast on the top of the water column. I suppose I could have tried to modify the worm but it is one of those things I never got around to trying. I did think about it many times, often saying to myself and a few of my clients that maybe someday someone would make a heavier plastic worm.

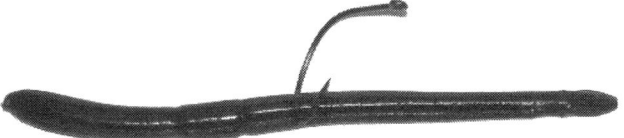

Wacky rigged finesse worm

Enter Gary Yamamoto the man behind the senko soft plastic stick bait revolution. The story goes that Yamamoto was trying to make something like the present day senko but had trouble working out the specifics. One day, he was trying to draw a picture of what he wanted for his plant manager when he looked down at a BIC ballpoint pen in his hand and realized that was the shape he was looking for. The rest has been bass fishing history.

Yamamoto made a mold from the BIC pen, and through the injection molding process included salt to add weight, and scent along with a few secret additives to make a soft plastic weighted stick bait. The senko would fall slowly through the water column and was irresistible for finicky largemouth and smallmouth bass. This was the bait that I was looking for, but little did I know that it would change the way I fish and be a Godsend for me and countless fishing guides across the country.

I had read a little bit about the senko on the internet but had not tried them until one of my clients pulled them out of his tackle box. He had been fishing for pre-spawn largemouth bass down in Texas. We were having a good day on the river as my clients were catching smallmouth bass on topwater baits and tubes. By mid-day the topwater bite stopped and smallmouth were just sucking on the tubes. We had already put enough smallmouth in the boat to make it a successful outing but I was hoping for more action.

One of my clients asked, "Have you ever fished with a senko before."

I replied, "No, not yet," since I did not know where to buy them except over the internet.

My client excitedly said, "I have a bunch of them. Do you think they would work in the river?"

My response was, "Don't know, never tried them. Go for it!"

He rigged up a white senko on a wide gap hook and made a cast over some mid-river rocks. He must have made about a half dozen casts and he said he was getting strikes but the smallmouth were dropping the bait. I told him to let the bait fall and when you feel a bite wait a few seconds before setting the hook. Following my advice my client started to catch a bunch of smallmouth. It did not take long for both his fishing partner and the guide to get in on the action.

We continued to catch smallmouth the rest of the afternoon and we were all having lots of fun. The only thing going through my mind was how I was going to get some of those senkos to use on the river for my clients for the rest of the week.

On the ride back to their motel, the only thing we talked about was this hot new bait. I told my client that the first thing I was going to do when I got home was to go on the internet and order a bunch of senkos. Since the cat had not yet gotten out of the bag and while senkos where no secret, they were tough to find on the shelves of local bait and tackle shops in the northwoods. I told my client that I wish I could get my hands on some for tomorrow.

I dropped my client off at the resort and after they paid me the guy with the senkos opened his box and said, "Here, take these since I won't have any use for them for a while." He gave me four bags of senkos and I could not have gotten a better tip.

Now I had a hot bait for tomorrow but I knew I needed more so the first thing I did when I got home was go on my computer and order a bunch of senkos. I don't remember what the amount came to but I do remember that it was more cash than I would have liked to have spent. After all, I did not know what colors would work best but most important of all, I did not want to run out of senkos.

For the immediate future I had to try to stretch my baits as far as I could. So the question was, should I start out the morning with senkos or start my client out with other baits? If I started out with senkos and we started catching fish right out of the gate I could be out of senkos by noon. So I decided to start my clients out with a combination of tubes, topwater lures, and soft plastic minnow baits and save the senkos in case the fishing got tough.

I got lucky, since on that particular day we started out with a great topwater bite and it stayed consistent throughout the day. About noon, either my clients were getting lax or the smallmouth were hitting the topwater baits light as my clients' hook percentage started to plummet. I was going to try a topwater bait but instead grabbed my rod with the senko and waited for one of my clients to miss a strike with their topwater bait.

I did not have to wait very long and a smallmouth nudged one of my clients' baits and whenI was sure that the bass would not return to the topwater bait I fired the senko at the smallmouth. A few seconds after it hit the water I felt my line get tight and then get slack. I did not know if the smallmouth were hitting the senko light or if they weren't getting close to the hook, which being Texas rigged was in the head of the senko. This happened to me a few times and I knew I had to do something different.

When I reeled in the senko, and looked at the wide gap hook if hit me. Why not hook the senko through the center like I usually do with the slider worm? The smallmouth became more aggressive on the topwater bite so I had to wait a while before one of them missed a fish. On the next missed smallmouth I again fired the senko with the hook rigged in the middle, and wham! I hooked the smallmouth almost instantly. Did I hook the smallmouth because I placed the hook in the middle of the senko or was the fish hooked due to the more aggressive bite? I will never know that answer. All I can tell you is that from that point on I would hook the senko through the middle about 75 percent of the time while fishing on the river. I can honestly say that I used the wacky worm set up with a senko before I ever heard or read about it.

Since those early days I have been on a mission to perfect using stick baits for river and reservoir smallmouth and have caught thousands of smallmouth. It is easy to use and works under most conditions making it the ideal method for a guide. The only problem that I have is that, just as with many presentations, clients tend to want to fish the bait too fast. I try to explain that the stick bait has a slow fall and it does not need much help from the fisherman, especially if you are fishing in any current.

Wacky rigged stickbaits catch big smallmouth

Stick baits are not the best bait to use during the pre-spawn since they are not a search bait. Not that smallmouth won't hit a stick bait in the spring but if pre-spawn smallmouth are scattered, which they can be on many occasions, you need to cover as much water as possible. Once you locate more than one smallmouth in an area, using a crankbait or jerkbait, they are an excellent follow up bait.

When using a stick bait in the spring, I have found that on most days smallmouth prefer a horizontal presentation. A wacky worm is a vertical drop presentation so it is less effective in the cold water associated with the pre-spawn. Texas rigging a four inch stick bait with a 3/0 or 4/0 wide gap worm hook will give it a more horizontal presentation. You can either drag the jerkbait along the bottom or let it fall vertically, but by twitching the stick bait you will keep the bait horizontally in the water column.

My most productive technique after I have located smallmouth is to cast out the stick bait and let it drop about half way in the water column. Next raise your rod tip about three feet, drop it back down and slowly reel in the slack which will move the bait horizontally about two feet. This will get the attention of the smallmouth and it will hit the stick bait as it sinks. If you don't feel a strike after the bait sinks about two feet again raise your rod. You can't work the stick bait too slowly in spring. When you feel a pick-up, wait a few seconds before setting the hook. A quick hook set will result in a missed fish. Again, the secret to success is patience.

If smallmouth are holding tight to the bottom or tight to wood cover you will need to the drag the stick bait along the bottom. This will take even more patience since a five pound pre-spawn smallmouth can bite like a small perch. Mix in a cold front and a drop in water temperature and you can expect the bite to be light. Since I don't like to add weight to a stick bait if at all possible this technique works best in water less than six feet deep. I don't worry about wind since I try to avoid wind when fishing for pre-spawn smallmouth. Areas out of the wind and in direct sunlight see warmer water temperatures.

When dragging the stick bait across the bottom it is critical to pause occasionally. About 80 percent of your strikes will occur on the pause. Just as with working the bait higher in the water column, the movement will get the smallmouth's attention. If the bite is light I will drag the stick bait about two feet and let it sit for as long as one minute. If the bite is more aggressive I will pause my retrieve about five or ten seconds. On many days one definite pattern is the longer the pause the larger the smallmouth. For colors I use minnow imitation and crayfish imitation colors.

One cold May Day I had two old codgers fishing with me. They had fished with me several times in the past during the summer and fall. Hearing my stories of all the big pre-spawn smallmouth my clients catch, they decided to give this pre-spawn smallmouth fishing a try. I told them that the fishing could be great but that in May inclement weather could put a damper on the fishing, unlike fall when a cold front can put big smallmouth on the feed bag. They fished with me one cold October day and caught a boatload of big smallmouth using red tail chubs.

They were familiar with stick baits since they had used them while fishing with me in summer. Before we got started I showed them how we would be hooking them Texas style with a wide gap hook instead of wacky style like in the summer. I knew where the smallmouth were holding so at least even with the cold front we would not have to search for them, although I was hoping that they were not holding too tight to the bottom. Not that they are not catchable when they are holding tight to the bottom but for anglers with marginal fishing ability it can make for tough fishing.

We tried fishing the stick baits higher in the water column but could not even get a strike. Finally, I decided to head for a favorite stump field that always held smallmouth during tough conditions. My clients made perfect casts, dropping the stick baits tight to the stumps. However, even though I kept stressing that they retrieve the bait slowly and give a long pause it was not registering. It did not take long for me to realize that this was not going to work.

I was thinking of what I could do next when I watched one of my clients trying to untangle a birds' nest. After I heard a few not so nice words he nicely mentioned that I needed to put new line on his reel. I did not say a word and just watched as he messed around with the line for three or four minutes before he untangled his mess. I am too nice of a guy to tell him that I had just respooled his reel the night before and that it was operator error! Finally, he reeled up the slack and yelled, "I got one!

Soon after his bone shaking yell I landed a 21 inch female smallmouth whose belly was about to burst.

The worst part about the whole thing is I could not get him to comprehend that the big smallmouth hit the stick bait because it was sitting motionlessly on the bottom. He thought that it hit the stick bait on his retrieve and he said that when he reeled in the slack he pulled the bass out of the stump.

On the next cast he went back to the fast retrieve and he went back to catching no bass. After a while, I became frustrated because I knew the smallmouth were present and I could not get my clients to slow down their retrieve. I was actually hoping for him to get a bids nest so a smallmouth might pick up the stick bait laying on the bottom, even if it meant that I would have to respool the reel again. I did manage to salvage the day by putting the stick baits away and having my client fish with leeches on a slip bobber. If that technique does not work you might as well put the boat on the trailer.

Whether you are fishing a river, reservoir or natural lake, fishing stick baits rigged wacky style is deadly for spawning smallmouth and largemouth. Just as with pre-spawn bass, having knowledge of spawning locations are essential. In clear water you will be able to sight fish and see the bass on their beds making it all the easier. When anglers can sight fish bass on a bed, they can drop the bait right in front of the bass' nose and catch fish like a pro. Although there are times when the fishing can be tough, for the most part if you are in the right place at the right time you will have fun.

While I do fish clear water lakes during the spawn much of my experience fishing a wacky worm during the spawn is on stained water reservoirs and rivers. Smallmouth can be very aggressive at this time but due to the limited water visibility anglers will need to spend more time searching for the beds. On some rivers and reservoirs smallmouth will return to the same spawning areas annually while on others, due to changing conditions, they will spawn in different areas. On most water every year is different so you will need to adapt.

When using a wacky worm the trick is to cover water effectively and not fish too fast. Smallmouth will not move to chase any bait and if you make your casts too far apart you can miss more fish than you will catch. Make your casts tight to the shoreline but no further than five feet apart. This will make your bait visible to the highest possible number of smallmouth. If you catch one smallmouth slow down and make casts close together.

Start out with a four inch stick bait and use either a #1 octopus hook or a #2 Eagle Claw Lazer Sharp L042 to hook it wacky style. Make a cast and when the bait hits the water, don't do anything for about five seconds, but keep an eye on the line. The slightest twitch in the line or movement in any direction will signal a pick up. Line is critical for this style of fishing especially if you are old like me and don't see as good as you used to. Later in summer smallmouth will hammer the wacky worm but in spring they are often just pushing the bait and if you depend on your rod to signal a strike your catch numbers won't be very high.

When you see line movement you need to be patient. Slowly reel in the slack and when you feel a tight line lower the rod tip and count to five. If the smallmouth feels any pressure at this point it can drop the bait. Next, slowly raise the rod until you feel pressure. If you feel no pressure, the smallmouth has dropped the bait. If you do feel pressure raise the rod with a slow steady motion and when the rod gets at the 11 o'clock position give it a swift pull.

If you are having trouble hooking fish switch to a three inch stick bait. Don't worry about changing colors because if the color you are using is already inviting a strike, a color change will not trigger a harder strike. However, when you downsize the bait the bass will engulf the bait as it moves it off the bed making it easier to set the hook.

I prefer to use a fluorocarbon/monofilament hybrid line or fluorocarbon line when fishing the wacky worm for river smallmouth. Over the years I have been able to do considerable research with different lines due to my clients' line choices. I have seen every kind of line imaginable in my boat and can compare the numbers of fish caught with each kind of line on a given day. My personal favorite is Yo-Zuri Ultra soft in mist green. While some anglers prefer braided line (and it will catch fish) I can increase my numbers with the hybrid line due both to the high visibility and limited stretch.

Many of my clients inquire as to what the ideal rod is for using a wacky worm. Although there is no definite answer since much depends on the cover you are fishing and whether you are after largemouth or smallmouth bass. For smallmouth I like a six foot six or seven foot medium light action rod with a fast tip. If you are fishing cover for largemouth bass you will want to use a heavier rod.

Don't make the mistake of just pounding the shorelines. Unlike a clear water lake where a smallmouth can come from a great distance to hit a bait, these stained water smallmouth have limited vision. A big female can be staging just off the spawning bed. If you just work the first few feet of the bank you will miss the big smallmouth. So after I am convinced that there are no bass tight to the shoreline I raise my wacky worm and let it drop in deeper water in hopes of finding a hawg.

Each year some of the largest spring smallmouth are caught this way. Just as when the male is on the bed, a wacky worm slowly fluttering downward can prove irresistible to a staging or post-spawn female. Again, watch your line since a big smallmouth can grab the wacky worm and sit tight. They are sluggish from spawning and are a bit lethargic. I have set the hook on what I first thought was a rock and it turned out to be a 20 inch smallmouth. Here again, in order to score you will need patience.

As far as colors go in stained water it is hard to beat watermelon red and green pumpkin with either copper or gold flakes. The flakes on the stick bait will illuminate in the stained water and resemble a crayfish. With the exception of white I seldom use a bait that is only one color in stained water. On some days white will be hot while on others you won't even get one pick up. If you are fishing with a partner have one person use white and the other a crayfish imitation bait.

Steve Kaehr with a pre-spawn smallmouth

After spawning is complete smallmouth can remain in the shallows as long as crayfish are present. Male smallmouth will be aggressive after they leave the nest and a wacky worm is the ideal presentation. Since these male smallmouth are aggressive they will grab the stick bait without hesitation, often moving it quickly to keep it from another male smallmouth. It is necessary to be prepared for strikes as soon as the bait hits the water. Watch for slack line, because it is common for a smallmouth to pick up the stick bait and head for deep water which means diving towards the boat. It is critical to reel in all the slack line before setting the hook, otherwise the smallmouth can drop the bait.

The only problem with rigging a stick bait wacky style is that they are a one fish bait. By hooking the worm through the center you weaken it. By the time you grab your catch all you have is the hook as the two pieces of stick bait fall into the water. In fact, the first year I was using senkos I was more concerned about saving the bait instead of getting the bass in the boat. These baits were too hard to come by to watch them fall to the bottom of the river. On more than one day we ran out of the hot color and that was almost enough to make a grown man cry.

So I quickly learned that while these baits are effective they are also expensive, and since I was using them on a daily basis I had to figure out something other than a surcharge for my clients. Well, I did not figure it out myself but one winter I was at a Sport Show when a tournament fishermen showed me how to place an O ring on a wacky worm. I went out and bought a bunch of O-rings and saved a ton of money the following year.

Shortly after that I started using the O-Wacky Tool produced by Case plastics. The tool goes over the worm and allows you to push the O ring onto the center of the worm with ease. This tool allows for the use of a slightly smaller O-ring than you can put on by hand. If the O ring is too loose it will defeat the purpose since you will need to skin hook the stick bait allowing it to break in half when you catch a fish. Case Plastics also makes a complete line of stick baits called Magic Stiks.

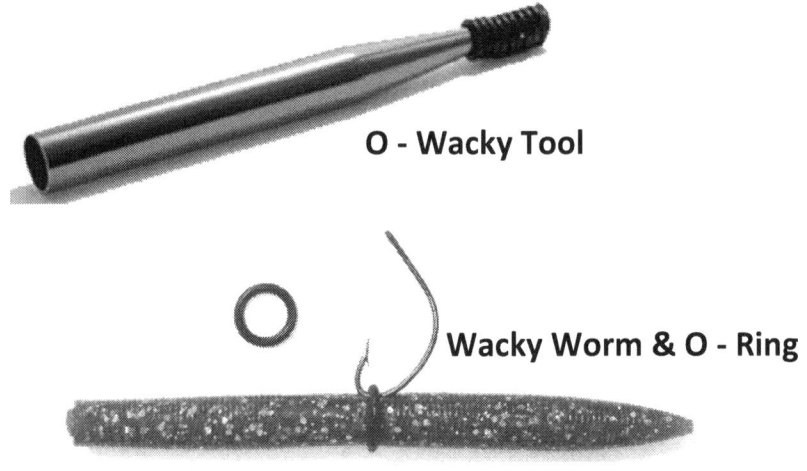

O - Wacky Tool

Wacky Worm & O - Ring

Another advantage to using an O-ring is that I believe that it increases your hooking percentage. With the hook more exposed, on the hook set the odds are higher that the hook will find the smallmouth's mouth. I have no statistics to back that other than just by observing the increased catch of my clients. My clients have a wide range of different levels of expertise and I believe that a more exposed hook has helped them all regardless of their ability .

In summer, the wacky worm is a staple for me when fishing for smallmouth on the river. This is where the wacky worm has revolutionized the way I fish. Prior to the wacky worm I would fish a variety of different techniques and usually find the best presentation for the day through trial and error. In a weeks' time I could be using several different techniques and on any given day one would out produce another. On most of my guide trips I usually start out at least one of my clients with a wacky worm while the other will throw a topwater bait or soft plastic minnow style jerkbait. On a typical day, it does not take very long for everyone in the boat to be throwing a wacky worm unless there is a good top-water bite.

One advantage to using a wacky worm is that it will catch river smallmouth in a variety of structures while other presentations might only work around one type of structure. I like to start out in the mornings fishing grass edges and will have my client cast tight to the grass. If the smallmouth are holding in the grass then I will switch to the same stick bait but I will rig it Texas style. After we catch all of the smallmouth in the grass we usually cast wacky worms tight to shoreline cover. If smallmouth are holding tight to cover I will have my clients tie on a weedless wacky worm hook. Many times by letting the wacky worm sink it will drop into the deeper wood which will hold the big smallmouth.

Even though a stick bait sinks, many times you will need to add some weight to get the bait down to deep cover. On windy days and in current a non-weighted stick bait does not sink very well. A few manufacturers make weighted hooks and jigheads for wacky worm fishing but I rely on weighting the stick bait. Since I already rig my wacky worm with an O-ring, I like to add a bit of lead to my worm to help it sink. What I do is buy a roll of plumbers solder and cut ½ inch to one inch strips and insert them into the center of the worm. This added weight will cause the worm to fall faster but won't impair the action.

This 6 pound smallmouth was found in mid river rocks

    I also fish a lot of mid-river structure in summer that is perfect for the wacky worm. This mid- river structure contains a mix of rock, logs, grass, and most of all, foraging smallmouth. Smallmouth can be sitting at different levels in the water column. Topwater baits can be hot at times but there are many days when they just will not rise to hit a bait on the surface. My records show that about 80 percent of the time I can catch smallmouth with a wacky worm so it is definitely my go to bait. The reason the wacky worm is so effective is its ability to drop to all levels in the water column. So whatever depth the smallmouth are holding, if they won't rise to strike a bait the wacky worm will find them.

    I will position the boat so I can drift slowly downstream with the head of the trolling motor pointed to the rear of the boat. I have my clients cast at a 45 degree angle up-stream. As the stick bait sinks, I tell them to reel in the slack and watch the line. Most of the time a smallmouth will hammer the bait and set the hook on its own. If no strike is detected and the stick bait drops to the bottom, I tell them to raise the rod and again let the stick bait sink. By the time the bait ends up behind the boat it is time for a new cast. This is a simple method and even novice anglers will catch fish. When river smallmouth are aggressive there is no presentation that can come close to this for sheer numbers. My personal favorite was a day when I and two clients boated 122 smallmouth with this method in one day.

I have caught smallmouth with the wacky worm on the river well into the fall period. They are particularly deadly during the early fall period which in the northwoods is September and early October. Smallmouth can scatter during the early fall period but, unlike spring, they are very aggressive and will move to strike a bait. The wacky worm is not the perfect search bait but it is an excellent follow up bait to a spinnerbait or crankbait.

September wacky worm smallmouth

The type of structure I am fishing will dictate the color. When fishing around rocks, until the water temperature drops below 60 degrees crayfish imitation colors are best. Once the water temperature drops below 60 degrees it is a definite minnow bite so I switch to white, pearl hologram or silver flake. If I am fishing around weeds all I use is the lighter colors.

Once the water temperature drops below 55 degrees I forget about rigging it wacky worm and opt to rig it Texas style. At this time the stick bait is most effective dragging it along the bottom. The same retrieve and pause technique used during the post spawn is effective. In fact, I still remember the day I caught a massive seven pound smallmouth on a stick bait on a miserable fall day.

We were fishing with red tail chubs on the edge of a creek channel and my client had caught several smallmouth over 18 inches. We were running out of chubs so I grabbed my other rod rigged with a four inch white stick bait on a wide gap hook. Just as I was getting ready to make a cast my client said that he had never fished with a stick bait in the fall. I told him that it is easy as long as you work the bait slowly. I made a cast and let the stick bait sink to the bottom and told my client to watch how I drag the bait along the bottom a few feet, pause and continue to drag the stick bait.

I gave the rod to my client and watched him rip the stick bait across the bottom. On the next cast I stressed that he had to slow the bait down and stop it occasionally. He slowed the bait down a bit and he did stop once but it was evident that my advice was not registering. So I took the rod and told him to play close attention to what I was doing.

My cast landed right on the edge of the creek channel, and I let it drop. I told my client to watch carefully as I raised my rod and dragged the bait about three feet. Then I paused and yelled to him that I had a strike. I set the hook and told him that it was a big fish, not knowing how big it was. Both of our eyes nearly popped out of their sockets when I lifted the massive 23 inch smallmouth into the boat. The smallmouth was in full fall binge mode and she hit the scales at seven pounds.

With that my client said in a humorous tone, "I guess I was not moving the bait slowly enough but I think I like fishing with chubs better since they leave more room for error."

That was the largest river smallmouth I have ever caught, and I guess I have my inept client to thank. The only question I had was why the big smallmouth passed up my clients' red tail chub since he made several casts in that area. Did the big smallmouth just move into the area or did it prefer the stick bait over the chub?

On natural lakes the wacky worm is effective for pre-spawn, spawning and post-spawn largemouth bass and can be fished in a similar manner as when you are targeting largemouth. The biggest difference is in my choice in stick baits and hooks. For largemouth I like a five inch bait with a 1/0 octopus or a 4/0 wide gap hook. Due to the size of their mouth it is easier to set a hook on a largemouth bass when they are spawning. My color selection for largemouth is also a bit different since they prefer natural colors like watermelon, green pumpkin and black in both clear and stained water lakes.

Boat docks are one of the most obvious forms of cover on any lake containing both largemouth and smallmouth bass. Many northern lakes that I fish are absent of cover and boat docks are the main attraction if not the only option besides searching for suspended bass or fishing deep weedlines. A problem can arise when fishing on weekends because boat docks are obvious bass cover and, in turn, get pounded. On heavily pressured lakes the stick bait is my bait of choice.

All boat docks are not created equal. In general, the bigger the dock, the better it is. Big docks will provide a lot of cover for baitfish and crayfish in addition to abundant shade for bass to wait in ambush. Some docks are surrounded not only by other boat docks but with cover such as brush piles which act as fish cribs attracting both bass and panfish.

While a series of boat docks will hold a lot of bass some of my favorite docks are longer off the beaten track. An isolated dock can hold a lunker since it might be the only available cover in a large area. Look for smaller bass to hold on the outer edges of the dock while the big bass will be laying tight to the back edge and will be missed by most anglers, so make sure you fish the entire dock.

For many anglers including myself, the wacky worm has replaced Texas rigged plastic worms and jigs when fishing docks. The key to fishing docks is casting accuracy. Generally speaking, the further under the dock the angler can place the bait and the closer you can keep it to the edges the more bass you will catch. On heavily fished lakes it is important to squeeze your bait into an area where few other anglers can place it. Accomplish this and you will be rewarded with a big bass.

When fishing stick baits around boat docks I rig them both wacky style and Texas style, with my choice depending on the dock and surrounding cover. On northern lakes boat docks need to be taken out of the lake in winter so portable docks with aluminum post and plastic or wood decking are the rule. These docks offer only limited cover and for fishermen snags are not a problem. Personally, I hate them! Give me an old dilapidated wooden dock any day since they hold a ton of bass even if you do get the occasional snag. On these snag free modern docks, wacky worms are the perfect presentation. If you are lucky enough to fish a lake with old boat docks then you will need to rig the stick bait Texas style.

During the dog days of summer a wacky worm will catch its fair share of largemouth bass on both natural lakes and reservoirs. On reservoirs I look for steep rock shorelines that contain downed wood. While wood and rocks in shallow water will also hold largemouth, they tend to be more aggressive along steep shorelines. Early in the day largemouth will cruise tight to the shoreline looking for crayfish. Cast the wacky worm on either side of the wood tight to the shoreline. Most of your strikes will be hard so be prepared. Later in the day I will let the wacky worm drop deeper into the water column as the largemouth bass move tight to the wood.

Early and later in the day, as largemouth cruise the weedlines a wacky worm is another option. On some days minnow baits or spinnerbaits will be the bait of choice, but if they fail to produce, try a six inch wacky worm. I will also use it as a follow up bait to a spinnerbait. Once you catch a few bass with a spinnerbait, even though they are aggressive they become gun shy. If you pitch a wacky worm along the weedline or in the middle of surfacing baitfish I guarantee you will get immediate results.

Stick baits, especially when they are rigged wacky style may not be a miracle bait but they sure have made my life easier, and I am sure many other fishing guides would agree. Along with catching fish you can now buy them everywhere. There is now a long list of manufacturers that make stick baits and finding them is no problem, even in remote northwoods bait shops. So if you run out, regardless of where you are fishing you can usually find a few bags somewhere. As far as which ones work best, I have seen most of them in my boat at one time or another and most of them work. Some are heavier and others are more durable.

Chapter
Jerkbaits

    I remember back in the early 1990's when Slug-Go mania engulfed the bass fishing community. This was supposedly the ultimate shallow water plastic. It could be worked on the surface like a topwater bait and at shallow depth ranges like a wooden jerkbait. In his wildest dreams Meridian, Connecticut bass angler and lure designer Herb Reed did not imagine the excitement this new lure with a unique design would create.

    The first time I saw one of these hot, new and odd looking baits at a tackle show I admit that I had my doubts. A plastic worm or a grub should resemble a crayfish or a nightcrawler, at least in the mind of a fisherman. The Slug-Go didn't look like any minnow I had ever seen swimming in the river. If it had not been for the fact that I had read so much about how many bass it was catching I would have given it a pass. The only regret would be that when I had my hands on them I should have bought more; because little did I know that, like all new hot baits, it would soon be hard to get your hands on one. However, unlike other new baits, other variations of the bait flooded the market almost immediately.

Original Slug-Go

The new generation of baits became known as soft plastic jerkbaits. These baits became known for their ability to entice shallow oriented bass, especially those cruising the banks, feeding on the flats, or those feeding or schooling near the surface. Although these bass are easy to catch, they receive heavy pressure and on some lakes can attract a crowd. Soft plastic jerkbaits can also be deadly for suspended and deep water bass.

Although these baits were originally fished weightless, recent innovations now offer hooks with weights molded onto them, in addition to special weighted inserts, to better allow the baits to be worked in deeper water or to better stabilize them in shallow water. Even today many anglers are unaware of the numerous applications and rigging techniques available for these versatile baits. They may use them extensively when bass are shallow in the spring, but don't give them a second thought for suspended or deep water bass. If an angler spends time fishing deeper water they will get to the fish that others pass up.

When retrieving these baits it is important to remember to avoid impairing the action of the bait. The most common retrieve is to keep the rod tip pointing towards the water. This serves to keep the line out of the wind and allows you to work the bait unimpeded by slack line. Use six inch sharp snaps of the wrists to retrieve the bait. When the fish are aggressively feeding on or near the surface, you will observe many strikes so keep the bait in site during the entire retrieve. I like to let the bait flip across the surface like a wounded baitfish when I notice bass feeding on the surface. Some anglers set the hook too quickly when they see the bass hit the bait, so seeing the strike can be a problem. Make sure that you feel the fish before setting the hook.

If the bass are hesitant about taking the bait near the surface try working the bait one to three feet below the surface. At this depth you will still be able to keep eye contact with it. To work the bait at this depth, just snap your wrist and pause, and after the bait sinks a few feet, again snap your wrists. Sometimes the bass will chase the bait and other times they will hit it on the drop and you will need to coax them to strike.

When bass are deeper, you may need to switch to stern weighted hooks or inset weights into the jerkbait. Weighted soft plastic jerkbaits are effective when you need a fast retrieve. A rapid retrieve will cause an unweighted jerkbait to dart out of the water. Although this may sometimes be the desired action, in most situations you want the bait to say under the surface.

Weighting your jerkbaits with insets and weighted hooks works fine and it is much easier if you use jerkbaits that will sink. My favorite jerkbait is the 3 ½ inch Case Sinking Minnow or 5-inch Case Sinking Shad. These baits are salt impregnated like a soft plastic stick bait causing them to sink. The problem when weighting a jerkbait or using a weighted hook is that you can have a problem getting the jerkbait to drop in the horizontal position. As it descends through the water column it will tilt slightly downward making it look unnatural. The salted Case jerkbaits horizontal drop is almost perfect, which will trigger more strikes.

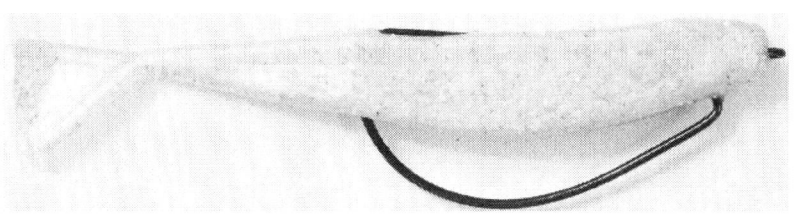

3 ½ " Case Sinking Minnow and 4/0 wide gap hook

Jerkbaits catch big bass spring, summer and fall

Current can also be a problem if the jerkbait does not have any weight added to it. Unweighted jerkbaits will hold near the surface and not sink. If bass are active they will hit the bait floating on the surface but in most instances they will refuse it. The ideal retrieve in current is to have the bait descend one or two feet below the surface making the Case jerkbait the ideal bait in current.

It is important to rig the jerkbait for both the water you are fishing and the level of bass activity, basically matching the retrieve to the mood of the bass. When bass are feeding and active, just about any way you rig the bait will catch fish. I have seen people hook the jerkbait in the strangest ways and catch fish. One day while I was guiding I watched a guy pull a four inch jerkbait from his tackle box but did not pay any attention to how he was hooking it. After a few casts into a patch of river grass he landed a 16 inch smallmouth. As I grabbed the bass I saw that he was using a number four live bait hook and it looked like he nose hooked the jerkbait.

While my client did catch a smallmouth at first I did not know what to say. I nicely explained that that particular bait was designed to be used with a wide gap hook, letting him know that the way he was rigging it would eventually catch him a clump of grass. He was responsive to my idea so I gave him a wide gap hook and he continued to catch smallmouth from the grass bed. I never did ask him why he was hooking the jerkbait through the nose when fishing the grass.

I first started using the original Slug-Go primarily for largemouth bass. Since most of my guiding is for smallmouth bass it did not take me long to start catching them as well. When smallmouth were cruising the shallows during the pre-spawn there were days when the Slug-go would catch the most fish. However, it seemed to be one of those baits on which you either caught a ton of fish or none at all. The newer plastics are much more versatile baits and the bite is much more consistent.

When it comes to catching numbers of pre-spawn largemouth bass it is hard to beat a soft plastic jerkbait. The only drawback to plastics is that they are not search baits and you should have an idea of bass location before using them. They are, however, my "go to" bait once I have established bass location.

My first choice in plastics for pre-spawn largemouth bass is minnow imitation soft plastic jerkbaits. These baits are especially deadly when bass are on the flats or just off their spawning beds. In the northern waters that I fish, five inch jerkbaits work best but in southern waters larger baits are more popular. If the water temperature drops or you are hit with a cold front, switch to a four inch jerkbait. I rig the five inch jerkbait with a 3/0 or 4/0 hook.

In spring, bass will often refrain from hitting a bait on the surface. Soft plastic jerkbaits will float so many anglers use weighted hooks. While weighted hooks will work just fine, I prefer to use salt impregnated jerkbaits since the salt will both cause the jerkbait to sink and stimulate a strike. Case Plastics makes the Sinking Salted Minnow and Salted Shad which are salt impregnated jerkbaits. There are several other manufacturers that make salt impregnated jerkbaits. The bottom line is that if bass are off their spawning areas you will need the jerkbait to sink.

Cast the soft plastic jerkbait and let it drop for a few seconds, then give it a few short twitches and then a pause. On the pause the jerkbait sinks and a bass will hammer the bait. I will vary my twitches and the amount of time I let the jerkbait drop until I find the right technique for the day. There is no set retrieve when using soft plastic jerkbaits. As far as color goes, I stick with white, silver flake or a color that imitates the preferred minnow forage in the water you are fishing.

Much of my experience with soft plastic jerkbaits for smallmouth is while guiding on rivers. In recent years this fantastic bait has enabled many of my clients, regardless of their fishing ability, to catch big smallmouth. Much like the soft plastic stick bait, the minnow style jerk bait will catch both high numbers of smallmouth and big fish on the same day. When I fish the stick bait rigged wacky style it has a vertical drop. The jerkbait rigged with a wide gap hook is a more horizontal presentation. So when you use both baits on the same day, by using baits that have a different drop, you can effectively fish the water column. Some days smallmouth will prefer a vertical drop and on other days they prefer a horizontal presentation. Eventually we find the preferred bait for the day.

Sinking soft plastic jerkbaits are excellent cold front baits during the pre-spawn. Cold fronts will scatter smallmouth and they are not eager to chase the bait. The jerkbaits allows you to cover water at a moderate pace and still work the bait slow. Don't snap your wrist but use a slow twitch to move the bait about six inches and let it drop. I will let the bait drop for about a ten count, slowly raise my rod and repeat the slow twitch. When fishing after a cold front, when I detect a strike, I wait a few seconds before setting the hook. I will occasionally add a rattle to the jerkbait too since the added noise will trigger a change in the mood of a bass. Sinking jerkbaits are so effective that I hardly ever use hard jerkbaits in rivers and reservoirs.

I have also had great success using soft plastic sinking jerkbaits on clear water lakes during the pre-spawn. The only problem is that on some days the smallmouth do not want to hit the bait when it is sinking. When you twitch the jerkbait a bass will follow but they can move away from the bait as it drops. Under this situation I switch to a hard plastic suspending jerkbait. On one particular day it made the difference between catching a few fish and many fish.

The lake I chose to fish that day has a series of small rock points scattered along the north shoreline. Although we had to deal with the cold front the northwest wind would not be a problem since we would be fishing tight to the steep bank on the north shoreline. After a choppy boat ride across the main part of the lake, once we entered the calm water on the north end of the lake I dropped the trolling motor and proceeded slowly to the first point. I assured my client that the smallmouth spawn on the points and that while the cold front may have pushed them off the spawning sites they would not venture too far.

My client started fishing with a crankbait looking for suspended fish. It took a while but he eventually caught an 18 inch smallmouth, but we were then hit with another dry spell. While he was working the crankbait I was fishing tubes, finesse worms, soft plastic stick baits and soft plastic jerkbaits. I had a few soft strikes on the jerkbait but that was it. I was using the same jerkbait with a weighted hook that was responsible for my clients catching over 60 smallmouth just a few days earlier. I watched the smallmouth follow the jerkbait and when I paused, the fish moved quickly away from the bait so I knew I had to change my game plan.

I tied on a suspending jerkbait and patiently fished at different levels in the water column. I had a strike, but not like the tail nip I experienced with the soft plastic jerkbait. A 19 inch smallmouth almost yanked the rod out of my hand when it smashed the jerkbait. After I released the smallmouth I gave my client a similar jerkbait and he started to catch smallmouth. That day may client caught about 15 quality smallmouth, which is not bad when fishing after a spring cold front. For what it's worth, one of my clients had fished a hard suspending jerkbait on my earlier outing on the lake and he did not catch one smallmouth. To be successful, you need to establish the bite for each particular day. You must know when to switch to a suspending jerkbait or continue to use a sinking soft plastic jerkbait. I keep stressing throughout this book that fine-tuning your presentation will catch more fish.

Once spawning is complete females will move away from the spawning areas and head for cover. River and reservoir smallmouth can hold tight to cover during the post-spawn but will attack an unsuspecting minnow that happens to swim too close to cover. A jerkbait will mimic baitfish and trigger a smallmouth to leave its comfort zone as long as the jerkbait drops down into the strike zone. Smallmouth won't rise too far up into the water column to strike a jerkbait so you will need to fish slowly and let the bait drop.

The 3 ¾ inch Case Sinking Minnow is the ideal morsel for a finicky post-spawn smallmouth. By Texas rigging the sinking minnow with a 3/0 wide gap hook an angler is able to cast tight to wood cover and let the bait drop slowly into the strike zone. I will let the jerkbait drop for at least 10 seconds, give it a slow short twitch and again let it drop for about 15 seconds. Post-spawn smallmouth can bite light so wait a few seconds before setting the hook. The slow vertical fall will get the attention of the bass and the horizontal movement of the bait caused by twitching your wrist will trigger the strike.

Patience is a virtue when fishing jerkbaits. An aggressive twitch of the rod might trigger an active smallmouth but it won't entice a neutral or inactive one. Many of the largest smallmouth I catch are taken by finessing the jerkbait. I will let the jerkbait sink, and with slack line I raise my rod about one foot and let it drop. I watch my line for any movement signaling that a bass has grabbed my jerkbait. When I see a smallmouth pick up the jerkbait, I slowly reel in the slack and set the hook when I feel the slightest pressure.

Patience will catch a big smallmouth

If you were to use a hard plastic suspending jerkbait, you might catch a smallmouth, but most likely you'd get snagged in the wood cover. This is one of the main reasons that I don't use a suspending jerkbait when guiding, since my clients always seem to find a snag. With the cost of suspending jerkbaits, this is a serious issue. However, if I have my clients tie on a sinking soft plastic jerkbait, they avoid the snags and catch fish. Even if they do get the soft plastic jerkbait snagged, the cost is minimal.

Minnow style jerkbaits are effective in all types of cover but shine when fished around wood cover and weeds. While soft plastic jerkbaits remain effective when smallmouth are relating to wood cover it is an essential part of my arsenal when fishing mid-river weeds. I use both floating and sinking jerkbaits when fishing river grass depending on both the current and density of the grass. If the grass is thick, I will use an unweighted jerkbait rigged on a wide gap hook and let the bait drift over the grass. Big smallmouth will hide under the grass on bright sunny days, similar to the way a big largemouth will find comfort under slop. Smallmouth will strike a surface bait, but the treble hooks will pick up grass before you even start your retrieve.

My technique is simple: as you drift downstream make a cast on a 45 degree angle downstream. With a high speed retrieve reel, reel in the slack and lower your rod tip and give the bait vigorous twitches. These erratic movements will look like surfacing baitfish feeding on insects or smaller baitfish. Keep the line as taught as possible and make sure you feel the fish on the line before setting the hook. This method has resulted in many 20-inch river smallmouth in summer. Although I prefer to move the jerkbait drifting over the weeds, I have had many of my clients catch smallmouth doing nothing but just allowing the jerkbait to drift. This will work as long as you keep a taught line to set the hook.

When I am guiding I will have one or both of my clients fishing over the grass with the unweighted jerkbait and I will work a weighted jerkbait like a Case Sinking Minnow or a wacky worm along the edge of the grass. This way we are able to cover the grass effectively and adapt accordingly. On a typical summer day on the river we usually use both presentations hand in hand.

During the early fall, river smallmouth can scatter as they forage on minnows so you will need to cover a variety of different types of structure. Unlike in summer where minnow style baits are not as effective around rocks as a wacky worm, they will trigger vicious strikes in the fall. As the water temperature drops smallmouth start to stack up and they continue to chase schools of minnows. When fishing in current I rely on the Case Sinking Minnow and Case Sinking Shad. If the jerkbait only drops a few feet below the surface you will be missing a lot of smallmouth. Your jerkbait should drop to a minimum of half way between the bottom and the surface to trigger a big smallmouth.

Fishing a soft plastic jerkbait along the edge of a creek channel or slough is the best way that I know to imitate a live red tail chub or shiner. Make sure you effectively fish the area working the top and mid sections of the water column. Cast the jerkbait rigged with a 4/0 wide gap hook right on the edge of the creek channel and close to weeds. Once the bait hits the surface I will give it a vigorous twitch then reel up the slack as quickly as possible in anticipation of a savage strike. If a bass does not inhale the jerkbait, give it another twitch and let it sink along the edge of the weeds and after about five seconds give it a few short twitches making sure your line is taught. Watch your line since a big smallmouth will head for deep water. If you see your line moving toward deep water reel in the slack before setting the hook. On one cold October day in 2011 my clients and I caught 12 big smallmouth on the edge of a small creek.

Creek channel smallmouth

The Case Sinking Minnow will also catch big smallmouth holding tight to the bottom. One trick I use in fall is to rig the jerkbait on a jighead and crawl it along the bottom. Use a weedless jighead due to the possible snags. I also use a long shank on my jighead to let the jerkbait lay as horizontal to the bottom as possible.

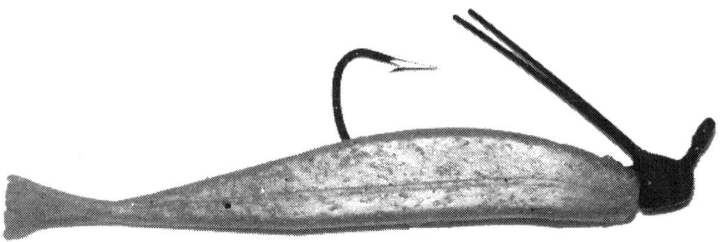

Jerkbait & jighead

Fishing a jerkbait on a jighead is also deadly when fishing deep holes and around dams. These are the areas where big smallmouth stack up in the fall. Smallmouth can be scattered throughout the water column so be prepared to fish all depths. Late in the fall I will toss out my anchor when I mark fish on my locator, so I can effectively fish the area. If there is a chop on the water and you don't use an anchor it will be hard to detect a strike. I like to use as little weight as possible.

Soft plastic jerkbaits will catch monster fall smallmouth in clear water natural lakes. While I don't fish them on a jighead as I do in rivers and stained water reservoirs, they are deadly when fished around weedlines. Just like when I was fishing the river grass in summer, it is important to fish both the weeds and the weed line. The Case Sinking Shad is my favorite fall bait for weed related smallmouth and largemouth bass. When fishing weeds I will work the Sinking Shad at a moderate speed looking for aggressive bass. When working the weedline, I work the jerkbait slowly and let it drop along the weedline. I catch big bass with both presentations.

As far as color goes, I seldom use a jerkbait that does not imitate a baitfish. Look in to my bag of tricks and you will find white, pearl, and white with silver and gold flakes. On occasion I will throw a natural colored bait like green pumpkin or watermelon on a clear water lake. When fishing deep clear water lakes, it is important to use fluorocarbon line, which will allow the jerkbait to sink to its maximum depth.

One issue some have with soft plastic jerkbaits is that they have trouble setting the hook. This is a result of the angler's poor choice of rod as opposed to their technique. Most anglers who complain about losing fish are usually using a light action rod with a fast tip. Anglers who have success fishing jerkbaits prefer a six foot six or seven foot medium heavy rod with a lot of backbone and spool their reels with braided line to eliminate stretch. This set up works in most types of water.

If you are fishing in clear water you might want to use fluorocarbon line. When fishing on the river for smallmouth and I am using a four inch jerkbait, I like to use a six foot six medium action spinning rod spooled with eight pound fluorocarbon/monofilament Hybrid line. When using five inch jerkbaits I use a bait caster but my choice of line will depend on how far in the water column I want the jerkbait to fall. By using 10 pound fluorocarbon line the jerkbait can be fished as deep as ten feet. If I am fishing over grass I will spool my baitcaster with braided line. So as with any plastic bait, your choice in line will be dictated by the type of cover and water depth.

The verdict is that soft plastic jerkbaits will not only catch lots of fish but big fish as well. Jerkbaits can be used spring through summer and can be fished in shallow and moderately fished water. Never leave the boat landing without them.

Chapter 7

Slider Fishing

Most of my bass fishing has been on northern lakes, reservoirs and rivers. While I have made a few excursions to southern reservoirs, they were short trips and my success was marginal. That is not to say that I have not learned a technique or two from anglers in different parts of the country. To this day I am always open to new ideas and for the most part bass are bass regardless of where they live. Some of my most effective bass patterns originated in other parts of the country, and all I had to do was to fine tune them to fit my home water.

By the late 1970's I had become proficient with the fine art of fishing plastic worms. Plastic worms were a deadly largemouth bass bait when fished tight to shoreline cover and weeds. They were no secret and they quickly became the rage in the 1970's. Due to their popularity prime bass structure was hit hard, especially by weekend warriors. In the 70's bass anglers did not have a wide selection of plastics worms to choose from and it was inevitable that a bass would get tired of looking at the same worm in grape or motor oil. While I enjoyed worm fishing, I did have one serious problem-- I could not figure out how to use them to catch my favorite fish, the smallmouth bass. Fortunately, things would change.

Sometime in the late 1970's I picked up a copy of Fishing Facts magazine and flipped through the pages, stopping when I saw an article on something called "Slider Fishing." The lead photo in the article showed a guy with a short spinning rod and a nice smallmouth with a small plastic worm hanging out of his mouth. As I started to read the article, I quickly realized that this was a revolutionary new idea. The main concept behind slider fishing was not about catching bass in shoreline cover and weeds, but instead catching bass suspending off structure and open water. After reading the article I was excited and couldn't wait to give this new technique a try. Little did I know it would open the door to a new way of approaching the waters that I fished.

Slider fishing was developed by Charlie Brewer. He developed the Slider system to fool black bass in what he called the "tough, mean" reservoirs of east Tennessee, southeast Kentucky and the Highland Rim of middle Tennessee. Brewer's Slider Worm launched the finesse revolution 20 years before it became popular. Although the southern reservoirs are much larger than small northwoods lakes they have many similarities which include clear water, low fertility and limited structure. Not to mention that they can also be tough and mean especially after a cold front.

Brewer returned home from World War II to Lawrenceburg, Tennessee and opened a radio and TV repair shop with knowledge gained in the South Pacific. A natural-born tinker, Brewer grew weary of the long, fishless hours throwing a baitcaster spooled with black nylon line and a crankbait. He figured there had to be a better way to catch bass more consistently when they aren't active and chasing lures.

Brewer developed a unique leadhead jig designed to plane the water, not fall to the bottom like a rock. He also poured his own 4-inch ringed worms with an egg sack that tapered to a paddle tail. He would cast these worms on a short graphite or graphite composite rod with a Tennessee handle for increased sensitivity. He removed the bail from the reels to increase casting distance for his 1/16 to 1/4- ounce leadheads and diminutive worms. He founded the Crazy Head Lure Company in 1970, which became the Charlie Brewer Slider Company.

The key to Brewer's system is presentation. The Slider method is designed to find bass suspended in the water column or holding just above the bottom. Bass in clear-water lakes suspend much of the time, especially during summer and early fall. On stained water lakes and reservoirs in the north, smallmouth bass will suspend off structure during summer and fall. Regardless of your geographic loaction, suspended bass are tough to catch.

The original Crazy Head was a flat-bottomed leadhead that came through the water in a straight line on the retrieve. Brewer later developed other styles of flat-sided heads and bullet shaped ones, but the concept remains the same. The heart of his Slider system is manipulating the speed of the retrieve and the weight of the leadhead until you hit the combination of depth and speed that the bass prefer on any given day.

In the Fishing Facts article Charlie Brewer explained how to fish his slider worms around structure. He would cast parallel to the structure and count to ten. Next, he would reel the Slider worm with a rhythmic but slow cadence and watch his line intently. He instructed anglers to keep counting down and reeling slowly until getting a rapid peck or a nip from a bluegill, crappie or small bass. This is the activity zone. Count down a little bit more and on the next cast you should catch a bass. Once you find the depth and the speed that you want, you can fish similar areas all over the lake and catch fish all day. Even though the Slider worm is a worm, it is designed to mimic a minnow.

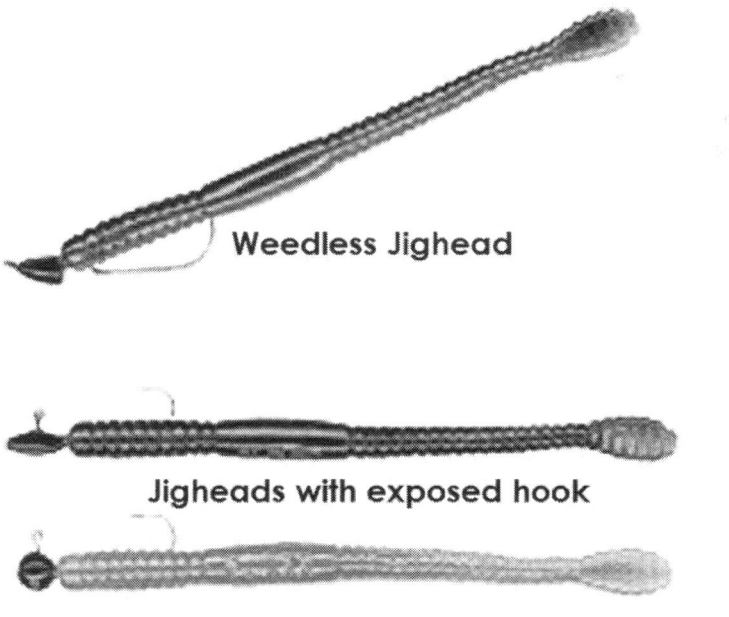

Weedless Jighead

Jigheads with exposed hook

After reading the article I did not hesitate to order the Slider Kit from an ad in Fishing Facts. When my package arrived, I really did not know what to expect. I forgot what I paid for the kit but my first reaction was that this stuff is not going to work. The kit was a small tackle box with five compartments: one filled with odd looking jigheads and the other four filled with small, 4-inch straight-tailed worms. The color selection was limited to black grape, motor oil and brown with an orange tail. Admittedly, I was skeptical, however, it did not take long for me to get a rude awakening and get my wheels a turning.

I was not living in the Northwoods at that time but had a real job down in the Chicago area. I could not wait for Friday so after work I could head north and prepare for a weekend on the water. Now this particular weekend I was really pumped since according to the magazine article I had the hot bait that was going to catch more and bigger bass. So after my usual Friday night stop at the local watering hole I slipped away early so I could be on the water early. Even though it was Friday night, there were fish to be caught and I could party another time.

Not one to waste time when it comes to fishing, I was on the water shortly after sunup and noticed a few other boats on the stained water reservoir but knew they would not be an issue since they were walleye fishing. The first place I fished was a rock point that dropped sharply from six to thirty feet. It was my favorite spot and I had caught several nice largemouth and smallmouth bass on the top of the point and a few walleyes on the bottom of the point. The problem was that if I could not catch bass on top of the point I got skunked. Jigging the deeper water with leeches caught an occasional smallmouth but most of the time I caught rock bass and a few straggler walleyes. When I did not catch bass on the point I would usually mark schools of fish suspending off the rock point but I assumed they were crappie.

The water was as calm as glass and I casted a floating Rapala over the rocks. I waited for the rings to settle and then I twitched the Rapala. After about ten minutes, I decided that there were either no bass present on the point or they were not interested in my Rapala. I tried a few other lures but eventually tied on a slider head jig with a grape worm. I did just like the article said: use a slow steady retrieve, which Charlie Brewer called a "do nothing retrieve." Well, either my do nothing retrieve was indeed doing nothing or I was doing something wrong. I tried all four colors and it did not seem to matter, so I couldn't blame the slider jig and worms since nothing else was working in my honey hole. It was about time to admit defeat and move onto another spot.

Suddenly I felt a slight breeze and it started to blow me off the point. This was before I had a bow operated trolling motor and I had to depend on a small transom mounted trolling motor to position the boat. It worked okay, as long as the wind was not too strong. I drifted off the point and continued to cast the grape plastic worm. After I drifted about 15 feet off the point I felt a tug on the end of the line. I tried to set the hook but there was too much slack in the line. I kept reeling in the slack and before I felt a tight line the water exploded and a huge smallmouth came flying three feet out of the water.

I got lucky since the big smallmouth inhaled the slider worm and once I finally reeled in the slack the fight was on. I continued to drift off the point and the smallmouth bull dawged and headed for deep water. Keep in mind that my experience catching big smallmouth was limited and being alone in the boat I had my hands full.

After drifting almost to the opposite shoreline I finally got the smallmouth into the net and unfortunately I had also attracted a crowd. The big smallmouth measured 20 ½ inches and I had never seen a smallmouth bass that big except on someone's wall. It did not take long for me to decide that I would be taking it to a friend of mine who was learning taxidermy. To this day that smallmouth sits on my wall and even though I have boated close to 900 smallmouth five pounds or bigger, it holds a special place in my heart. Not to mention that the rock point remains one of my favorite fishing spots.

A couple of guys in the other boats asked me what I had caught the big smallmouth on and being my pre-guide days, I told them the truth. When I told them I had caught the smallmouth on a Slider worm, they gave me a bewildered look. At the time I was more concerned that they saw where I had caught the big smallmouth. So it was obvious that I could not return to the point even though I knew there were more smallmouth waiting to hit my grape Slider Worm. Those two boats followed me the rest of the day and while I caught more smallmouth, the gawkers broke my concentration. I ended up putting my boat back on the trailer by 11:00 AM because, after all, I had bragging rights.

I now had a new weapon in my arsenal and for a number of years I caught lots of big smallmouth bass on Slider worms. I continue to catch suspended smallmouth bass off points and off-shore humps. The only aspect of Slider fishing that did not fit into my style of fishing was the use of the five foot rod. I might still have a five foot rod buried somewhere in my basement and in all fairness I did give the short rod a try, but even with light line I never did get the desired casting distance. I believe that this was mainly due to the stiff action of the rod. The short stout rod might work below the Mason-Dixon Line, but this Yankee could not make it work.

The one thing I embraced for many years was the Tennessee handle. The Tennessee Handle is a cork handle without the reel seats. Without the reel seats the angler is able to place the reel in the desired location to balance the rod, giving the angler the ultimate sense of feel. The proper location of the reel will allow the angler to place his index finger on the rod blank allowing him to feel even the slightest twitch from the blank. This technique has enabled me to out fish anglers using standard fishing rods under tough conditions with a variety of finesse lures. I would even use a Tennessee handle to fish light jigs for walleye. Unfortunately, due to extreme usage all my rods with Tennessee handles eventually broke and very few rod manufactures sell rods with Tennessee handles.

My favorite rod for casting Slider worms was a six foot medium action Lamiglas rod with a Tennessee handle. It was much easier to cast than a five foot rod. The only problem came when one of my clients stepped on the rod and broke the tip. Even though the Lamiglas rod has a limited lifetime warrantee, the rod was out of production and could not be replaced.

While I never caught a boat load of suspended smallmouth while using a Slider worm on a jighead, I caught lots of big smallmouth. It has been my experience that in northern waters you will catch one or two big fish on the first couple of retrieves. I don't know if you just catch the aggressive bass or if the other bass are turned off by the hooked smallmouth. On several occasions I would return to the spot an hour or so later and catch a few more big smallmouth.

That particular point is on a stained water reservoir but I have had great success fishing small rock points on deep, clear, natural lakes. One 800-acre lake I fish has two rock points, one on the north end of the lake and one point on the west end of the lake. Both points drop into 30 feet of water. The point on the north end of the lake is slightly larger and the surrounding rock shorelines break sharply into deep water. The point on the west end of the lake is adjoined by tapering sand shorelines were good weedlines develop.

Big fall smallmouth caught with a Slider Worm

In the spring both these points are popular fishing spots. They are loaded with smallmouth and most anglers have no problem catching them. I avoid the lake on weekends due to the heavy fishing pressure. The good news is that by mid-June when spawning is complete most of the bass fisherman are gone. In summer you will find a considerable amount of boats on the lake but most of them are chasing walleyes or panfish. Even though the angling pressure is for other species, the overall fishing pressure can cause smallmouth to develop a serious case of lockjaw.

Bass anglers who fish the lake in summer concentrate on shoreline wood, deep weeds and the one rock hump in the center of the lake that everyone knows about. While this wood, weed and rock pattern does produce smallmouth at times the fishing can be tough, but few bass anglers spend much time trying to figure the lake out. While it might not be my favorite lake to fish, thanks to Slider worms I was able to connect the dots and identify a few patterns.

Downed wood is everywhere and when you launch your boat you can put down your trolling motor and start fishing. Due to the clear water you can see smallmouth cruising the wood choked bottom in 25 feet of water. This can make for some tough fishing. However, on this particular lake you can forget about fishing the deep wood since by late June there are usually schools of suspended smallmouth cruising anywhere from five to 10 feet below the surface. These suspended smallmouth are easy pickings for a Slider worm.

This suspended smallmouth hit a Slider Worm

My pattern on this lake is simple; I either cast a Slider worm on a weedless slider head towards the wooded shoreline and a regular Slider head looking for suspended smallmouth. What usually happens is we catch largemouth bass from the wood and smallmouth over open water. It is a predictable pattern until mid-day. When the action slows I will move over to the weeds and cast Slider worms along the weedline.

If there is a chop on the water I will leave the shoreline and the weeds to other anglers and head for the points searching for suspended smallmouth. I have been fishing this particular lake for over 25 years and I have learned that a slider head with a black or grape four inch worm is the easiest way to catch a bunch of smallmouth. Smallmouth will suspend about forty or fifty yards out from the points and are usually suspending about five to ten feet deep in the water column feeding on baitfish. I have never caught a smallmouth over 16 inches but have caught as many as 30 smallmouth off one point. While I catch my fair share with grubs, tubes and crankbaits, the Slider presentation works best.

It is an easy pattern to tap into. If the wind is out of the south or southwest, which is common in summer, head for the point on the north end of the lake. If the wind is out of the east or north which is rare in the summer, the point on the west end of the lake attracts the most smallmouth. The only problem is that an east or north wind is usually the result of a cold front so the bite can be tough. This is where patience and concentration win the day. The slower you retrieve the slider worm the more smallmouth you will catch.

The rock hump in the center of the lake is also a great spot to look for suspended smallmouth. The only problem that I have when fishing the hump is dealing with walleye fisherman who flock to the hump when there is a chop on the water. In fact, on a few occasions I had to refrain from fishing smallmouth due to the over-abundance of walleye fishermen. But the day I remember most was when there were about a dozen walleye anglers on top of the hump and I was the only boat fishing for smallmouth. The good news was that the walleyes weren't biting but my client was catching a boat load of smallmouth.

We were catching smallmouth consistently from the weeds and shoreline wood when about mid-day the wind started to kick up. The smallmouth shut down and we could not get a strike. Even the points were like fishing in a dead sea. I knew that the only chance I had to put fish in the boat was to head for the mid-lake hump, knowing that I would have to deal with the walleye fishermen.

The hump is five feet below the surface and I told my client that the smallmouth usually suspend 10-30 yards off the hump and five feet below the surface. We were using 1/4 ounce jigheads and black worms with chartreuse tail. I told my client to make a cast and count to seven as I held the boat off the edge of the hump with my electric trolling motor. On the second cast my client caught a nice 16 inch smallmouth. After my client caught his second smallmouth I got into the action and we lost count of the number of suspended smallmouth we caught, but it was easily over 20. After my client caught about 10 smallmouth, he said that he had been watching the walleye fishermen and that he did not see one walleye caught.

Eventually the smallmouth action stopped and on cue, the walleyes started to bite. We had brought some leeches along in case the bite was tough. All we had to do was tie on a leadhead jig, tip them with a leech and move in for the kill. So before leaving the hump we got into the walleye action and my client and I ended up with a bonus walleye dinner. Now that, my friend is the ideal day on the water.

I have caught more suspended smallmouth with Slider worms than any other presentation in summer. In fall, whether you are fishing a point or a hump, suspended smallmouth continue to hit a Slider worm but crankbaits are more effective. When fall smallmouth hit a crankbait the school will follow the hooked smallmouth back to the boat. However, when I catch a suspended fall smallmouth on a Slider worm I seldom see a school of smallmouth following the hooked fish. This is an interesting observation. The only explanation I have is that the smallmouth see the crankbait in the hooked fishes mouth and just as with a live minnow they go into a frenzy. I have seen this happen many times over my many years on the water.

Slider worms also work well for largemouth bass that are suspending off wood cover in stained water reservoirs. This became evident one Saturday when I was guiding for largemouth bass on a 1,200 acre reservoir. The client wanted to fish for largemouth bass and only wanted to use my services for a half day. He had fished for smallmouth bass with me a few times and wanted to try something different. On the ride to the boat landing we talked about the minor cold front that had passed and how it could potentially affect the fishing.

After we launched the boat the first place we headed was to a beaver hut right around the corner. My client said, "I thought we would have to go for a boat ride." I replied, "No sense going any farther than we have to."

I put down the trolling motor and told my client to flip his six inch plastic worm along the edge of the beaver hut. He made more than one good cast but the results were the same, no bass. He made one more cast and his rod buckled over and the drag started to scream. We were both hoping for a big bass but when the line broke and we saw the wake we both knew it was a muskie.

I looked at him and said, "I guess we need to go for a boat ride. "

Since I always try to avoid fishing in the slop I hoped we would find some largemouth bass relating to the wooded shorelines. The only problem was this same wood also could hold a few hungry muskies, especially since we already had one bite-off.

We fished one of my favorite shorelines for largemouth bass and while we had a few bumps neither one of us was able to set the hook. Along with plastic worms we were using spinnerbaits and shallow running crankbaits. If it would have been 10 years in the future I am sure I would have been using soft plastic jerkbaits. However, we used what we had at the time.

My client opened up his tackle box and picked up a purple four inch Slider worm and rigged weedless on a Jighead. It did not take long before he brought a chunky largemouth bass into the boat. After that bass I told my client that we were going to return to our starting point so that we could work the entire shoreline with the Slider worm.

It turned out to be a fabulous morning especially after a cold front. My client landed about 15 nice largemouth bass. He would cast the worm, let it fall, and when the line became slack, which signaled the worm had fallen into the wood, he started the famous "Charlie Brewer do nothing retrieve "I also got into the action after I switched to a Slider worm. While we did not catch any big largemouth bass I can honestly say that if we did not make the switch to the Slider worm we might not have caught many bass that day.

I must he honest when I say that I don't use the Slider worm as much as I should. Why, you ask? I guess with so many plastics available on the market it is easy to forget about past success. However, every once in a while when nothing seems to work I can count on the Slider Worm to catch as Charlie Brewer often said, "One of Those Old Brown Fish."

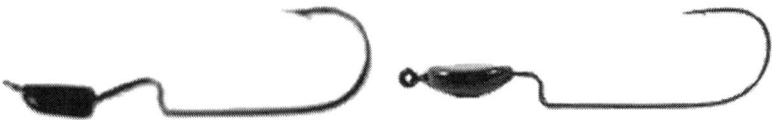

Weedless Slider Heads

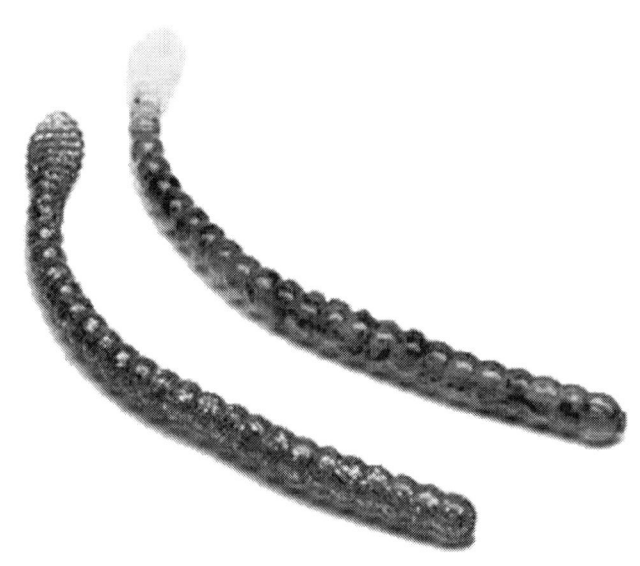

Chapter 8
Mojo Rigs

Most innovations in the bass fishing industry are the result of bass anglers trying to adapt to the needs of local fisheries. Sometimes a hot new bait never seems to catch on beyond local waters since they only work in specific situations. More often than not, a technique developed in one geographic location will usually work in another. Tight lipped anglers will try their best to keep a secret but when something catches fish it is inevitable that somebody will talk. One such innovation that was kept secret in Southern California was the Mojo Rig. The original Mojo Slip Shot fishing sinker is designed to drag the weight over the bottom and through deep grass. The long cylindrical design of the Slip Shot has less points to catch grass and cover while fishing and it can be easily positioned and secured anywhere ahead of the bait.

The Mojo Lure Company began in 1984 in Southern California and like so many other entrepreneurial hopefuls it started in a garage. With limited resources and a localized cliental the company was able to keep above water. Not only were they able to survive but expand after twenty years in the competitive fishing tackle industry. Today Mojo products can be found in the tackle box of both the bass pro and weekend warrior.

By the mid 1980's the deep clear water reservoirs in California were producing world class largemouth bass. These lakes were not hidden wilderness lakes but they were close to highly populated areas. So if you take a clear water reservoir and fill it with an army of educated anglers all trying to catch a world record bass you end up with highly educated bass, especially the big ones. In order to be successful on any water an angler needs to be one step ahead of the competition. If you expect to rely on luck to catch a big bass go buy a lottery ticket.

Most of the big bass caught from Southern California reservoirs were caught by live bait fisherman. These trophy hunters would use light lines, tiny splitshot sinkers and fine wire hooks. If there was any resistance in their presentation, the big bass would refuse the live bait. If they were that finicky with live bait, good luck trying to catch a trophy on artificial bait. With live bait not being fair game in tournaments, anglers had to emulate the finesse tactics of the live bait fishermen. This required the use of light line and small natural colored plastics with the use of a small tiny split shot instead of live bait. The problem that faced tournament anglers was when the split shot was clinched on the light line it would weaken the line causing the line to break. The original Mojo Slipshot was an advancement over the splitshot sinker which was pinched on the line. A Mojo Slipshot uses rubber strands to cushion the line from weakness. Although called the Slipshot, most anglers know it as the Mojo Rig.

Although they were long the staple of tournament anglers in Southern California it took years before they caught on back east. It had a surge in popularity across the Northeast and in parts of the South, but even today it is relatively unheard of in the Midwest with the exception of a few tournament anglers. If it were not for reading an article in Bassmaster Magazine back In 1999 I would have never heard of a Mojo rig. The first time I saw these sinkers I knew it was something that had to work.

While I only occasionally use the Mojo Rig while guiding, I have used it successfully on some of the deep clear lakes that I fish. Although it was developed for largemouth bass the Mojo Rig is excellent for catching smallmouth bass. In the northern waters that I fish the Mojo rig seems to work best when smallmouth bass are holding tight to deep sand grass. Before I adapted to the Mojo Rig I would catch an occasional smallmouth from the deep sand grass but I had to use live bait, just like on those California reservoirs. Not that there is anything wrong with using live bait if you are not fishing in a tournament but it is more challenging to use plastics. I caught an occasional smallmouth or two, I just could not develop what I would consider a definite pattern with any artificial bait. My verdict was that the bulky sinkers that I was using, while they were easily dragged through the sand grass, looked too unnatural in the clear water environment and the presentation allowed me to catch only one or two aggressive smallmouth.

When smallmouth are relating to weedline higher in the water column a little activity will often stir the pot and trigger a feeding frenzy. However, the deep sand grass is a whole other universe. Sand grass related smallmouth are inactive and although they are catchable you need to do a bit of attitude adjustment. It is necessary to drag a morsel right in front of their nose, and there is precious little room for error. The Mojo rig has turned a tough situation into a reliable fishing pattern.

The only snag with the Mojo Sinker was not the weeds but in trying to fine tune the rig with the proper weight sinker. Finding the right Mojo weight is not easy and will require much patience and experimentation before hooking a wary smallmouth. If the weight is too light it won't get the rig to the bottom and if it is too heavy and it creates too much of a ruckus going through the weeds, you will spook the school. It is to the angler's advantage to start with a lighter weight and go to a heavier weight instead of starting out with a heavy weight. If the weight is too light you will ride over the bass but there is a possibility that you will coax a smallmouth to ride up and strike the rig.

Rigging up a Mojo Rig is easy. All you need to do is slide on a sinker and tie on a 1/0 wide gap hook and peg the weight to the line. The rubber pegs made by the Mojo Tackle Company work fine but they are expensive so I will use a toothpick to peg the Mojo sinker onto the line. Next, select your bait of choice and slide the pegged weight up the line to whatever leader size you desire. There are a number of plastic that can be used with the Mojo Rig when working deep sand grass for smallmouth bass. I prefer to use cylindrical jerkbaits like Yamamoto Senkos and Case Magic Stiks, four and six inch finesse worms and lizards. When working grass, or any other cover for that matter, it is important to Texas rig your plastics. If you are fishing an unobstructed bottom you can use an octopus hook.

Experience has taught me that smallmouth can hold tight in the grass and even the best electronics won't pick them up. I suggest that if you are on a good smallmouth lake that you fish the grass anyway, even if you don't mark smallmouth on your electronics. If I were to only fish for smallmouth that I marked, my prediction is that there would be many days when I would either get skunked or put only a few fish in the boat. This is one lesson that I learned the hard way over the years.

After locating a patch of sand grass I position my boat into the wind and use my electric trolling motor to move me slowly over the sand grass. When there is a heavy chop on the water I forget about the sand grass and look for smallmouth elsewhere. If you drift with the wind what will happen is the boat will drift too swiftly over the sand grass and it will be impossible to find the proper weight. Even if you do find the proper weight, it won't be in the strike zone very long and you will also have trouble detecting a strike. Even for a very skilled angler this can be challenging.

Once I position my boat over the sand grass I cast my Mojo rig into the wind and let it slowly drop into the grass. Be prepared for a quick strike because a suspended smallmouth can strike the rig on the drop. Once the Mojo Rig is on the bottom slowly lift the tip of your rod and let it fall again, reeling up the slack in your line. The slower you can work this rig the better. If you are not getting any strikes, crawl the rig slowly across the bottom. I have even caught smallmouth dead sticking a Mojo rig, which resembles live bait fishing.

A few rod manufactures have developed specialty rods for fishing Mojo Rigs. Most Mojo Rods have medium or medium heavy power and have a fast or medium fast action. They are either six foot six or seven feet long. A good Mojo Rod includes Fuji reel seats and premium cork split slip handle for weight reduction plus direct blank contact for helping you establish both feel and balance. I prefer to spool my spinning reel with fluorocarbon line.

In recent years, I have used a version of the Mojo rig to catch river smallmouth in summer. I ran across this presentation one day while joking around with one of my clients. We were catching lots of smallmouth on four inch Case Magic sticks rigged wacky style. Everyone was in a great mood since we had boated over 50 smallmouth and it was only noon.

As the boat drifted down the river and my client ate lunch, one of my clients jokingly asked when we were going to start catching the big smallmouth. I knew he was only kidding but he did have a point since we did not catch one smallmouth over 17 inches.

I said, "All the smaller fish are hitting our wacky worms before they get a chance to get down to the big smallmouth. I think we need to add some weight."

River smallmouth caught with a Mojo Rig

I had tried the new wacky worm jigheads and adding weight to the worm. This added weight does allow the bait to sink but if a bass does not strike the worm before if hits bottom snags can be a problem. But I had a hunch that the real big bass were in eight feet of water in the deep rocks. In order to catch the big bruisers we needed to not only get the bait down deeper in the water column, but keep it there without getting hung up. This is easier said than done.

When my clients relax that is when I get down to some serious fishing. So I fumbled through my bag of tricks and pulled out a box that had some Mojo Slip Shot weights. I grabbed a 1/8 ounce sinker and snipped off my wacky worm. I placed the sinker on the line and tied on my wacky worm, pegging the sinker about two feet from the hook. I held up the rig and said to my clients, "The smallmouth are hitting on wacky worms so let's see if this works."

I could tell that neither one of my clients had ever seen a Mojo sinker before and for all I know they probably thought that it was something I concocted. I explained to my clients that the Mojo sinker was developed in California and that I had used it successfully on a few clear water lakes but never on the river. Buy explaining that the Mojo sinker was perfected in California I had myself covered if I did not catch a smallmouth. Who would expect something that caught fish in a faraway place like California would work on a river in northern Wisconsin.

It was mid-summer and the river was at typical summer water levels: low! The current was minimal and by turning the head of my bow mounted trolling motor toward the stern of the boat, I could slide slowly downstream. This enables the angler to keep the bait as vertically with the bottom as possible. I works great when casting wacky worms over mid river rock structure. Now all I had to do was figure out how to apply the Mojo sinker and wacky worm to our plan of attack.

I had lots of experience in dragging tubes and knew that this would produce big smallmouth, but I wanted to try something different. However, I knew that the same dragging technique would work with other baits. I slowly dragged the Mojo sinker across the rocks and after the boat drifted about 30 feet I commented to my clients that, "Even if this rig does not catch any smallmouth it does not get snagged in the rocks."

One of my clients caught a nice smallmouth on the wacky worm and before I could comment on his fish, I yelled, "Fish on"

My client yelled that my fish was bigger than his as we watched the smallmouth jump three feet out of the water. While a guide never wants to catch a fish larger than his clients, this time was an exception since I was experimenting with a new technique. My client's fish was 16 inches and mine was 19 inches.

I offered one of my clients my rod so they could try the Mojo rig but they declined since they were afraid they would get the bait snagged. However, after I caught the second big smallmouth one of them said that they wanted to try the new rig. I rigged one up on his rod, explaining to him that all I was doing was dragging the sinker over the bottom.

While my client was experimenting with this new presentation, I shook things up a bit by nose hooking the worm instead of fishing it wacky style. As I dragged the nose hooked worm over the rocks I watched my client hook into a big smallmouth. About that time the other client yelled, "Where is my Mojo rig."

For the next hour both my clients caught smallmouth out of eight feet of water on the Mojo/Wacky rig and I caught nothing on the nose hooked worm. My clients inquired as to why they were catching smallmouth and I wasn't. I theorized that when the wacky worm was moving along the bottom it had more resistance than the nose hooked worm therefore it triggered more vicious strikes. While the sinker did not get hung up in the rocks it would occasionally jar the worm and that is usually when the strikes occurred. We never had strikes when the worm was dragged uneventfully across the bottom. This was the opposite from the stealth weight dragging through the sand grass on the clear water lake. While a bulky sinker might attract more fish in the stained river water it would also get hung up more often.

I don't use the Mojo/Wacky rig much but on a few occasions it has produced big smallmouth when other presentations catch smaller fish. Why it produces larger than average fish I can't say for sure since I am still in the experimental stages with this presentation for river smallmouth. Deep water finesse presentations can be modified to accommodate shallow stained water rivers.

Another shallow water application for the Mojo Rig when fishing rivers or reservoirs is when fishing stumps. Stumps are notorious for attracting both largemouth and smallmouth bass. During the post-spawn and after a cold front bass can literally push themselves against the stump. Without the use of a shovel or dynamite it can be impossible to pry them out. There have been a few days when I wish I could have had a stick of dynamite, not to catch fish but to wake up my inattentive clients.

Under these extreme circumstances bass can be gun shy and just like when smallmouth are holding in deep sand grass, if the right presentation is not used you can do more harm than good. So while the Mojo Rig is effective, you have to do everything just right. The first rule is to use a short leader. By pegging the sinker one foot from the hook you are less likely to have the worm wrap around wood or get caught in a crack within the stump. Next, cast tight to a stump and let it drop. Do not attempt to start your retrieve until the bait hits the bottom. Once you are on the bottom let the rig set for as long as one minute. If you don't feel a strike start a slow retrieve and do not shake the rig. Unlike with other presentations I have found that any aggressive movement can cause bass to totally shut down.

The Mojo Sinker is the only sinker that along with being almost snag proof will allow me to drag a bait through the wood without creating a disturbance. Prior to using the Mojo Sinker I used to place a split shot about one foot above the hook. While it did the job most of the time snags were a problem. If the Mojo Sinker gets hung up all you need to do is shake it loose. You might not catch a fish, but you won't lose the rig.

I have had my best success with higher profile baits as opposed to small finesse worms in summer. This is due both to the warm water temperatures and the dark stained water. A six inch plastic lizard or a six inch stick bait rigged weedless on a 2/0 or 3/0 hook will catch both smallmouth and largemouth bass. The larger baits will often eliminate strikes by smaller bass. In spring I use smaller baits.

The Mojo Lure Company makes the "Rock Hopper" which is designed to be ultra weedless and can be fished through almost any type of cover. You can slide or drag this weight and your favorite bait through rock, timber and brush. An angler can Carolina Rig or Texas Rig a Rock Hopper weight since the pivoting action of the cylindrical weight effectively reduces the amount of snagged fishing weights. I have not used the Rock Hopper but it sounds like another excellent sinker.

Mojo Sinkers

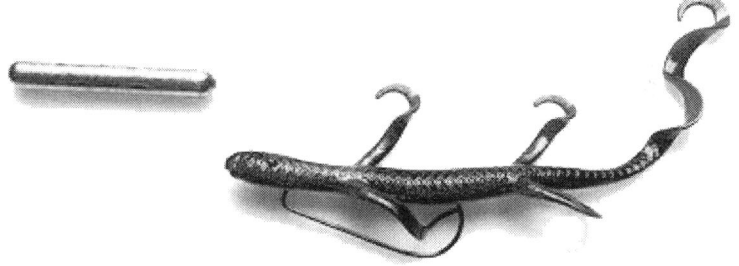

Mojo sinker and lizard

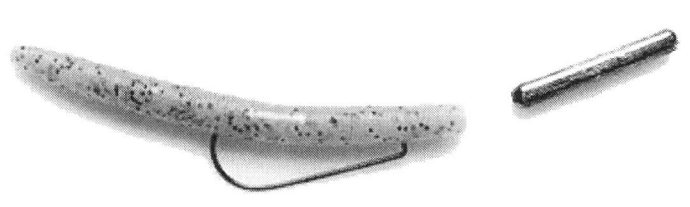

Mojo sinker and stick bait

Chapter 9

Drop Shot

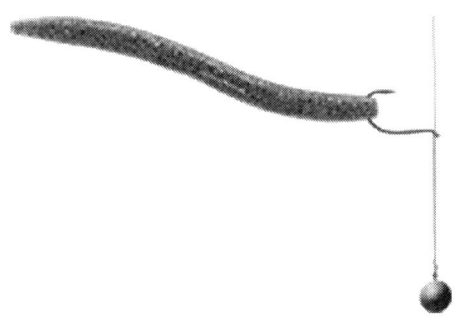

    The drop shot rig has received a lot of attention, due largely to its success in the western states. Unlike most west coast techniques which are home grown, the system has roots in the eastern United States. It dates back to the mid-70's, and was first seen in *Fishing Facts* magazine. I remember reading the article but while it sounded interesting it seemed too complicated at the time. I was not alone since even after national exposure it failed to catch on until the Japanese anglers resurrected the method for use on their highly pressured waters. The Japanese refined the technique and it soon returned to the States.

In 1997, drop shotting was relatively unknown, except to a few Southern California fishermen who had ties to Japanese manufacturers and pros. The system worked extremely well, and those that knew about it did their best to keep it a secret. Then, in winter 1999, two major tournaments were won using the drop-shot rig - the B.A.S.S. Invitational at Lake Oroville, and the WON Bass Classic on Lake Cachuma. Once the proverbial cat was out of the bag it spread like wild fire across the country. It is amazing how popular a rig can become after it wins a few major tournaments. If it were not for bass tournaments, bass fishing would still be in the stone age.

From the beginning, drop-shotting has been viewed as a vertical or near-vertical presentation for bass suspended generally at depths of 15 feet or deeper. The most significant characteristic of this method is the power of the drop-shot rig during times when bass are suspended off the bottom and are unwilling to hit lures on the fall. By adjusting the distance of the lure to the weight (sometimes referred to as the "leader," although it is not a leader in the traditional sense), an angler can hold a bait at these mid-depth levels indefinitely; basically putting the lure in front of the bass and leaving it there.

Drop shotting is not a technique that is difficult to learn and I have found it easy to teach it to anglers with limited fishing experience. For the most part the bites are hard and easy to detect. If the bass does not strike the bait hard, it will usually push the line off to one side so the angler has to be alert. This is an advantage to using visible line like Yo-Zuri H20. This 100 percent fluorocarbon has a slight green tint that lowers the reflectivity of the line below the surface of the water. However, above the surface of the water the line has reflectivity which allows the angler to see even the slightest line movement. H20 is a very soft fluorocarbon line that will cast easily and have less memory than other fluorocarbon lines.

Choosing the right rod and reel combination is also essential and there is no combo for all types of waters and situations. Most anglers prefer to use a rod with a fast tip for shaking the lure, and a reel that has a high gear ratio, so that if a bass is in cover, you will be able to get him out quick. Both six foot six and seven foot rods are popular but most pros rely on seven footers. Many rod makers have rods specially designed for Drop-shotting.

When choosing a reel, get one with at least four ball bearings, as this will ensure maximum smoothness. Purchase the best reel that you can afford. Since I back-reel and don't rely on the drag at all, it's of no consequence to me. However, if you depend on the drag, make sure the drag is smooth before you purchase the reel.

Just about any small, soft plastic lure will work for drop shot fishing. Keep in mind when choosing your baits that drop shotting is a finesse tactic and low impact colors, those that don't stand out from their surroundings, aren't likely to alarm or intimidate the bass and are therefore the most logical choices. On the waters that I fish, watermelon or green pumpkin are good colors. As far as the style of bait goes, my favorites are a four inch Weenie worm and a Case four inch drop shot worm. Through trial and error you will be able to find the right bait that mimics the baitfish on your favorite water.

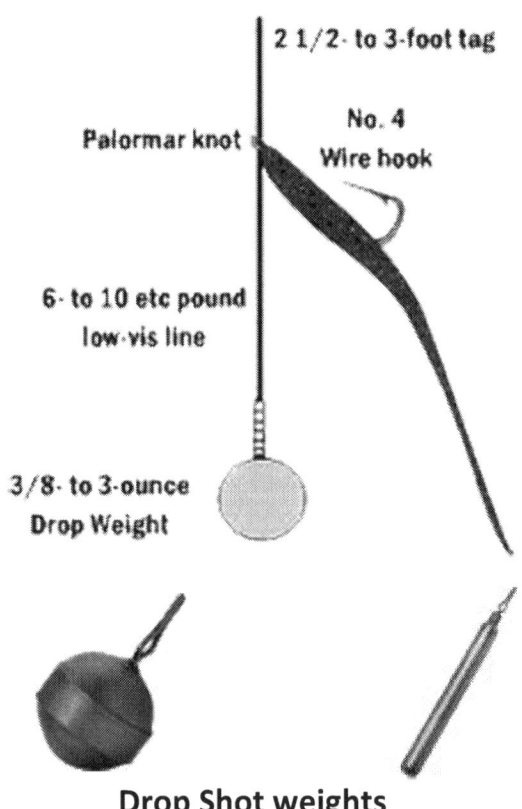

Drop Shot weights

One key aspect to drop shotting is the length of the leader or line that extends below the hook to which the weight is attached. When fishing rock or mud banks, anywhere from 6 to 18 inches of leader is appropriate. If you are fishing a lake with lots of weeds or deep grass make the leader long enough so the worm is above the weeds and the bass can see it. By dancing a worm over the weeds you give the bass an irresistible offering.

Drop shotting is very effective on deep, suspended bass. If you locate a school of bass suspended on deep structure with your electronics, position the boat over or near them and drop the bait right on top of them. Shake the worm keeping the weight on the bottom with some long pauses and work the area carefully. When dealing with suspended fish you will need to pay extra attention to the length of the leader and you will need to change you leader length throughout the day.

Some anglers have trouble comprehending that they are fishing when the line is slack. The sooner they understand this concept the more fish they will catch. As you move the rig along the bottom letting the line go slack between your shaking, and before feeling the weight on the rod tip, you have to anticipate a strike. Every time you move the sinker ever so slightly, look for any line movement. If you sense something, stop and work the bait in place as long as you can.

I have learned a few ways to fine tune drop shot techniques on the clear water northern lakes that I fish. Many of these lakes also have trout that suspend at all different levels in the water column. The smallmouth suspend off the bottom and can be very tough to catch. While drop shotting is very effective there are occasions when if everything is not right it won't catch fish. When the smallmouth are suspending off the bottom set the drop shot leader a bit longer. This will enable you to jiggle your worm just above the smallmouth. It is important to always place the bait right above suspended fish, because they tend to feed upwards.

Prior to drop shotting I had one lake where I would just hammer the smallmouth in the spring but after spawning I could not catch them with anything but leeches. I would drift the leeches in 20 to 25 feet or water and catch lots of smallmouth. I would occasionally catch them with plastics but if I was guiding it got to the point that all I would bring along was a bucket full of leeches.

This was one of the first lakes where I experimented with drop shotting. The night before I was going to take a few clients to the lake I rigged up a drop shot rig on one of my rods. My plan was to wait until my clients had caught a bunch of smallmouth with leeches and then pull out the drop shot rig to see what would happen. I was really desperate to figure out a way to catch summer smallmouth on this lake without using leeches.

Well, everything was going just fine since my clients were catching a lot of smallmouth; in fact, if anything they were catching too many since I was running out of leeches and it was only lunch time. The fact that I had never used the drop shot technique before made me doubtful that I would be making expert drop shotter's out of my clients. I was just happy that they had caught over 75 smallmouth on leeches even though the leech pile was running low.

I pulled my six foot six rod with the drop shot rig out of my rod storage locker and looked through my plastics for a small finesse worm. Keep in mind that this was in 1999 and not many anglers knew about this magical technique. One of my clients looked at my rod and inquired as to my experience with drop shotting. Never being a very good liar, I said that I had never tried it but since every bass magazine was exploiting this new technique I decided to give it a try.

I told my client that I did not have much for weights but I had a lot of small plastics that would work.

My client said, "I have a box full of weights, hooks and plastics. I spent two days this winter fishing with a guide in California who was an expert at drop shotting."

Never being one to claim to know everything about fishing, I replied, "Talk to me!"

As we drifted across the lake my client showed me how the California guide rigged up his rod and even gave me some of the four inch worms that they used to catch largemouth bass. After my client rigged up his rod and I rigged up mine we motored back to the suspended smallmouth. The other guy in the boat decided to keep using leeches since we did have a few left and, after all, they were catching fish.

There was a light chop on the water and I positioned my boat effortlessly over the smallmouth that were suspended two feet off the bottom. I decided to just sit back and watch my client since he had done this before. I opted to watch and learn. I could have played the "know it all" card and just started pretending to be an expert on a subject I knew nothing about but I had too much common sense. After all, I wanted to see this drop shot technique catch fish.

It took a while but eventually my client swept his rod and it became evident that he had caught a smallmouth. After he caught his second smallmouth it was time to give it a try. Due to my seven foot quality rod I could feel the weight on the bottom. It took a few weird movements of the line and I caught my first drop shot smallmouth. My client caught more smallmouth than I did that day but I was quite happy to see him catching fish and equally happy that he shared his expertise with me. By the way, his friend continued to catch smallmouth the rest of the day with leeches.

It was an interesting day on the water. The only thing we were doing differently was that we were using monofilament line which has a lot of stretch. Since I had done my share of walleye fishing, using a lighter hook set was no problem. We were also using a similar hookset that we used when a smallmouth would hit a leech. At that time I had never had any experience with fluorocarbon line. That would soon change as I continued to experiment with drop shotting. I guess that under certain circumstances a guide can learn a few things from a client!

Drop Shot Smallmouth

By adding drop shotting to my arsenal not only could I add this lake to the list of summer smallmouth waters but I was able to add a few others as well. The only complaint that I had with the technique was that it was so simple a concept it bothered me that I hadn't thought of it myself!

On my day off I will often head for a new lake. By fishing a new lake I will often be able to add the lake to my guide list, but it is also a challenge. On one late June day I decided to head into Michigan and fish a 300 acre clear water lake. I knew the lake had both largemouth and smallmouth bass present but I did not know which bass was the dominate specie.

After launching the boat I do what I always do on a new lake, idle and watch the locator. I idled around the lake and could not mark any structure let alone fish. Finally I came across a shoreline point. The point was in about 30 feet of water and dropped sharply to a depth of 50 feet. One side of the point dropped sharply and the other side of the point was tapered with scattered areas of gravel mixed with large boulders.

As I watched my electronics I was marking fish suspending about one foot above the boulders in 30 feet of water. The first thing I did was drop out a few floating markers over the boulders that held fish. I was excited and I was hoping that these fish were smallmouth and not walleyes. Not that I have anything against walleyes but I did not have any live bait with me and I doubted my plastics would catch them.

I was certain that this was an ideal drop shot situation. I positioned the boat perpendicular to the point and the rocks and pointed into the wind. It is important to keep the boat pointing into the wind as this allows you to control the speed of your drift and keeps the bait in the strike zone longer. I dropped the drop shot rig with a watermelon four inch finesse worm and allowed it to sink to the bottom. Once it hit bottom I let it sit several seconds and then gave the rod a few twitches. Once I got the rhythm I started to catch smallmouth. I repeated this procedure around the other rocks and again had satisfactory results. Had I not used the drop shot technique I might not have caught any fish that day and might never have returned.

Using the right hookset is also of great importance. Many anglers prefer the "reel set" to see the hook rather than the traditional "rip the lips" hookset. The sharp light wire dropshot hooks will penetrate easily with light pressure and you risk breaking the light line on a heavy bass with a hard hookset. A 'reel set" just means you reel in line as you lift the rod, all in one motion creating a steadily increasing pressure on the point of the hook instead of quick, sharp, line snapping jerks. If you buy cheap equipment you will be sorry since you will probably end up with a broken rod.

Drop shotting is not just a vertical presentation. A horizontal presentation involves "dragging" the rig along the bottom. Any time you want to add action to your bait while working it just off the bottom a drop shot is a great choice. The rig is usually flipped or pitched 15-25 feet to the target letting the rig drop to the bottom. After jiggling the bait in place on a semi-taunt line, you then slowly drag the rig closer to your boat a foot or two at a time. This seems to work well on largemouth bass that are less active.

Another horizontal drop-shot technique that works well for me on a 125 acre lake that I fish is to allow your line to go slack after moving the rig forward and jiggling the bait on this slack line for a few seconds. Then weight the line, that is, tighten up on the line to see if you feel anything different. If you do, then set the hook. If not, lift the sinker and move the rig a bit closer while repeating the process. I don't know why, but while it works on this lake I have not caught a bass on other lakes using this technique.

If I am fishing a lake that has big smallmouth I will try some creature baits, like a brush hawg. The wider profile of the creature bait will attract larger than average smallmouth and trigger vicious strikes. You will need to tie a wide gap hook onto the drop shot rig. I usually start out with a smaller finesse bait and switch to a creature bait once I have established the bite. Green pumpkin and watermelon are my favorite colors in clear water.

While I use my share of plastics, being a guide it is no secret that when things are tough I switch to live bait. I also deal with families and when you have a couple of young kids in the boat drop shotting in deep water is not an option. However, if the fish are in deep water you need to make an adjustment. On more than one occasion while fishing a clear water smallmouth bait, modifying a drop shot rig with a live leech has been a life saver.

I have also modified the drop shot rig for fishing with kids for river smallmouth. When I spend time on the river with kids in summer, it comforts me to know that river smallmouth like to eat nightcrawlers.

Drop shot largemouth from a Northwoods lake

My typical pattern is to find some rocks that I know are loaded with crayfish that will   attract a bunch of hungry smallmouth. Even under the toughest conditions I can produce smallmouth for my clients.

For a lot of years the problem was not in locating smallmouth but figuring out how my young client with little or no experience could catch a smallmouth before they became snagged in the rocks. After trial and error, without realizing it I had developed a modified drop shot rig.

What I would do is tie a Palomar knot with a number four Eagle Claw live bait hook which has barbs on the shank. I would leave a tag line about 12-14 inches long and tie an overhand knot up about three inches from the end of the tag line. Next pinch a slip shot weight above the overhand knot. To complete the rig I would hook a healthy nightcrawler either through the nose or the middle of the crawler. I found out hooking the crawler in the middle works best for kids since they don't throw the crawler off on the cast, at least most of the time.

The rig can be either set in a rod holder or fished with a slow retrieve. The knot on the end of the tag line helps keep the split shot on. If the rig gets hung up in the rocks the spilt shot breaks off and the split shot can be easily replaced. It is much easier to pinch on a cheap split shot than keep replacing hooks. This rig also tends to allow the crawler to ride a few inches off the bottom triggering more strikes.

I have also had good results with this rig using grubs and plastic worms when the smallmouth are holding in six to eight feet of water. I cast the rig upstream and, holding my rod tip high, try to keep as much contact with the bottom as possible. You will need to experiment with different split shots until you find the right weight. If you get snagged up in the rocks, no big deal since all you need to do is replace the split shot.

This can be a deadly presentation if smallmouth are holding tight to rock in heavy current. There are days when dragging a tube just does not get the job done. Instead of using one large split shot I will clinch on three or four in a series. This seems to slide over the rocks easier than one big weight. Using a three or four inch curly tail grub, I cast the rig perpendicular to the boat with the boat anchored and use a slow steady retrieve.

Drop-shotting has proven to be effective by thousands of anglers all around the globe. It is considered a finesse technique involving light line, light weights and small plastic baits. Whether anglers are fishing in highly pressured waters or remote Canadian Shield lakes, when the fishing gets tough drop shotting will put more fish in the boat. It should be a tactic in every bass anglers' bag of tricks.

Chapter 10

Shaky Head Fishing

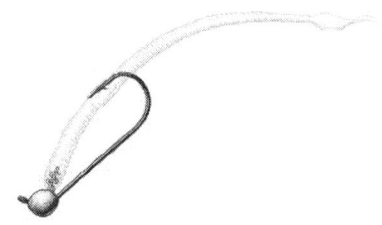

Most finesse worm presentations originated on the west coast. Those deep clear water reservoirs were indeed a tough nut to crack. Once the western anglers honed their skills back home, they brought these presentations to the south. When the west coast anglers started to win tournaments in southern impoundments attitudes began to change. It did not take long to find a few spinning rods spooled with light line in every angler's rod box.

Once southern anglers began using finesse presentations eventually someone would develop a technique to fit their home water. It was also inevitable that bass which were caught and released would become a bit skittish when they were bombarded with an array of big, gaudy baits fished on heavy line. When there was money involved, somebody would figure out how to catch these gun shy bass.

Not all finesse worm techniques came from California. One technique called Shaky Head fishing, originated in Alabama. The tactic was originally designed to catch cantankerous spotted bass that tend to avoid shallow water. Spotted bass are not found in the northwoods so my knowledge of them is minimal. However, I do know that they prefer deep water and often suspend, so I can equate some of their habits to smallmouth bass.

Shaky head fishing was a guarded secret among touring pros until Kevin VanDam won the Elite 50 tournament on lake Lewisville, Texas. He shattered the lake record with a giant 11-pound, 13-ounce largemouth bass. VanDam used the technique in his next three victories, but he wasn't alone. It became a go-to technique for a number of pros. For many pros, this technique has saved the day on more than one occasion. Whereas Shaky head fishing is best suited for rocky bottoms, sandy flats or around grass beds, it can be fished around the edges of thick cover and in water from 3 to 40 feet in depth. The one place to avoid fishing the rig is around thick weeds.

Shaky Head fishing involves a straight tail finesse worm rigged in a small, ball head jig. There are two ways to rig a shaky head on the jighead. The first is to Texas rig it, with the hook point all the way through the worm but just under the skin. This way works best when fishing weeds or cover. The other way is to push the point completely through the worm so it is exposed. This is the preferred method when fishing open water situations. I feel that the exposed hook will give you a better hook-set.

Choose your jig sizes on the basis of water depth, going as light as possible. Sizes 1/8 to 1/4 ounce are preferred. Most anglers prefer a jighead with at least a 3/0 size hook when fishing a six inch worm. A common problem with this rig is the worm tends to slide down the shank of the hook. To remedy that, bite off the tip of the worm, add a touch of glue, and push it flush against the jighead. Some jig manufacturers have added a tiny barb to the base of the jig that also will help hold the jig in place.

Once rigged, the angler makes a long cast and allows the bait to fall. The angler needs to be alert since a strike can occur in the first few seconds after the bait hits the bottom. If a strike does not occur, begin shaking the rod tip in short, rapid bursts, maintaining some slack in the line while you hold the rod in a 10 o'clock position.

Most anglers use worms that are from four to seven inches in length. When choosing a worm make sure it is both durable and buoyant. Berkley makes a worm that is perfect for shaky worm fishing. It is scented and it forces the bass to hold on to the worm a bit longer, which allows the angler to set the hook. Some finesse worms can be tough to rig up on shaky head jigs so there is no one size fits all.

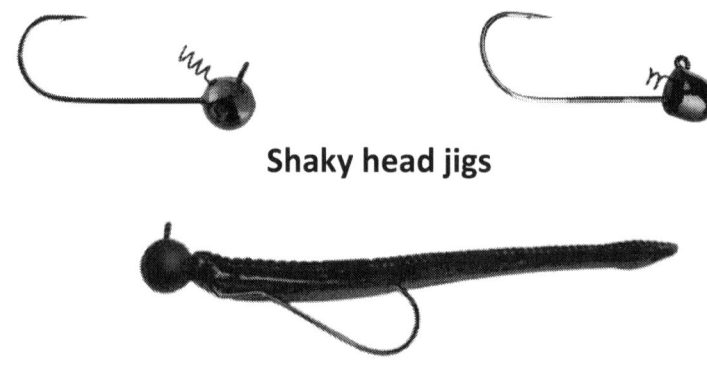

Shaky head jigs

Shaky head jig and worm

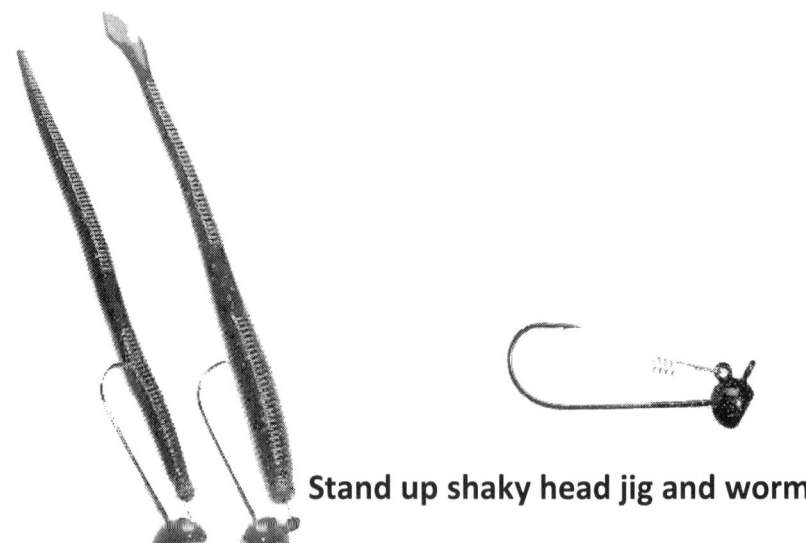

Stand up shaky head jig and worm

Although the shaky worm can work at any time, the preferred time to use the Shaky worm is during the post-spawn period or during summer cold fronts that can shut down an aggressive bite. Some anglers say shaky worms are best in clear water but others do well with it in stained water. In the south they use the rig while fishing rocky bluffs in winter. It is also an excellent rig for duping a bedding bass.

The proper rod and reel is essential when fishing a shaky head worm. A good rod for shaky worm fishing is a 6' 6" or 7' medium light action rod with a fast tip. Even though the rod should have medium action, it is critical that it has a strong butt to enable sweeping hook-sets. Many rod manufacturers make rods designed for shaky head fishing. Make sure your reel has a large arbor since you need to use fluorocarbon line. The smaller the spool the more memory fluorocarbon line has. Besides being more sensitive, fluorocarbon line will allow the shaky head worm to sink.

I have occasionally experimented with the Shaky worm on a few clear water lakes. On one lake in particular I would always find largemouth bass holding in 25 feet of water off the edge of a deep weedline. Since this lake had no smallmouth or walleye, I always assumed that they were largemouth bass. After reading a few articles on fishing shaky worms I felt that this lake would be as good as any to test this technique. So on my day off, I headed for a lake a few miles from my house to see if this technique worked.

First, I fished a soft plastic jerkbait over the weeds and caught two nice largemouth bass. Once the weed bite stopped I moved out to the deep water and located what I hoped was a school of bass. I tied on a shaky head jig and rigged up a watermelon six inch finesse worm.

I tired jigging the worm and for the first fifteen minutes I caught nothing. At first I did not know if my lack of success was due to my poor presentation or if the fish I was seeing down there on my locator weren't largemouth bass after all. I continued presenting the worm differently hoping to make this system work. Finally, I hooked a bass!

The best motion I found was to move my forearm an inch or two while keeping my wrist stiff. What I was doing was taking up the slack when I moved my forearm up and releasing it again when I moved my forearm down. What I had been doing was flexing my wrist and using too much arm movement. This was moving the worm too far away from the fish on the lift.

I fished the area for about one hour and caught four more largemouth bass with the largest one probably weighing around five pounds. I don't mean to make this sound too complicated but it has to be just right. The angler has to understand that their goal is to leave the lure shaking on the bottom in one place until you are ready to move it, not before. You shake the line which subtly gives motion to the jig and worm in place. You should not actually be moving the worm across the bottom! This may not be the best technique in my bag of tricks to use while guiding.

The shaky head worm technique also works on deep summer smallmouth bass as I found out on a stained water reservoir. Again, what does a guide do on his day off? He goes fishing! Time on the water spent in solitude is the perfect situation to experiment with a new technique. I was surprised at the results, not so much that it worked for smallmouth, but that it caught bass in stained water. Everything I read about fishing the shaky head worm was centered on clear water applications.

On this reservoir there is a rock pile that surges out of 30 feet of water and tops out right at the surface. It is prime area for smallmouth bass and if the conditions are right, an angler using plastics or live bait will find plenty of action. However, in the dog days of summer, which usually means bright clear skies and no wind, good luck. You might find a few smallmouth on the rocks at sunup but for the most part they move out to deep water during the day.

About 50 percent of the time I find these summer smallmouth holding within one foot of the bottom over a sand and rock bottom adjacent to the dam. I had caught several big smallmouth over the years drifting with leeches, and with those largemouth bass that I had caught with the shaky worm fresh in my mind I was armed and ready. I am always searching for ways to catch summer smallmouth from this particular reservoir without using live bait.

It was a typical August day with bright sun and no wind. I rigged up a 1/8 ounce shaky head jig with a six inch black finesse worm. I chose a black worm since I knew that smallmouth would inhale a black leech. I positioned the boat over a school of smallmouth and dropped the bait straight down. As soon as the worm hit the bottom I noticed my line moving off to the side and with a sweeping motion set the hook. In a few seconds a huge smallmouth went flying out of the water right in front of the boat. Needless to say I had already made my day after I released a 20 inch smallmouth back into the reservoir. I don't know why, but about 90 percent of the time when I catch a big smallmouth, whether it is in shallow or deep water, it seems as if it is on the first cast that I make in an area. After I catch a few smaller smallmouth I seldom catch a hawg.

Northwoods smallmouth like shaky head worms

As I repositioned the boat and dropped the shaky worm back into the stained water, I was certain that when the big smallmouth hit the leech it was sure it was hitting a jumbo leech. On my second cast I could not coax another smallmouth but shortly thereafter I had another pick up and boated an 18 inch smallmouth. I had developed a pattern and I was glad there were no other fishing boats in sight. The only people on the water were pleasure boaters and jet skis, and they had no interest in what I was doing.

My next stop was a steep rock ledge on the deep edge of a point. The top of the point is in five feet of water and the ledge drops to 28 feet. There are several sharp edges on the ledge and I knew from experience that summer smallmouth hold tightly to the bottom as well as on the granite ledges. I was determined to catch smallmouth on the shaky head jig.

I positioned the boat well out in deep water and made a cast along the granite ledge. I did this several times and did not get any kind of response. I do not have a "side finder" fish locator which will shoot a perpendicular signal from the transducer, enabling the angler to mark fish on ledges. Thus I was unable to establish whether the ledges held any smallmouth or if they were just refusing my presentation.

Although I was unsure of the status of the smallmouth on the ledge, my electronics showed that there was a full house at the base of the ledge. The instant the shaky worm hit the bottom I had a pick up and I set the hook into what would be another 18 inch smallmouth. They were thick on the base of the ledge and I caught four big smallmouth on four consecutive casts. I was starting to like this shaky head worm fishing.

When was I battling my last smallmouth a passing boat stopped. They saw the big smallmouth and the first thing out of one of their mouths was, "What did you catch it on?"

They knew who I was and knew that I guided on this reservoir. Since I had already divulged one of my hot spots I did not know what to say. Finally I said, "A shaky head worm." I am sure they were thinking, "What on earth is a shaky head worm."

I caught a total of 18 smallmouth on shaky worms that day and all of them were over 17 inches. While I was surprised that I caught that many quality smallmouth what really shocked me was when I hooked a 22 inch walleye. I knew when I hooked the fish it was not a smallmouth but who would ever think that a walleye would hit a shaky worm? I guess that there is a first time for everything. By the way, I did appreciate the walleye that night for dinner. As a matter of fact, this presentation might be worth considering if you are a walleye fishermen.

Shaky head worms do not work well in rivers unless you find smallmouth out of the current. I have experimented with it on a few occasions and while it will catch a smallmouth, there are many other presentations that are far more productive.

Fishing shaky head worms does not work on all waters but they should be a part of every bassers arsenal. It will take a bit of practice to perfect but spending time learning this deadly presentation will be worth the effort. I would suggest taking a few days each year and work exclusively with this fantastic presentation.

Chapter 11

Doodling

Bass trends come and go throughout the years and many people have emerged as leaders in the sport of bass fishing. None of these seem to have risen to fame so quickly as California professional bass fisherman Don Iovino. One of the things for which Iovino was most well known was his method of fishing, known as "doodling".

Doodling is a technique that is used on clear or slightly stained waters. While the water does not need to be crystal clear, you need at least two feet of visibility or more. That's because doodling is a visual presentation. The technique is also most successful when bass are holding at depths deeper than 10 feet. Because of the vertical presentation your boat will be directly over the bass, and if you are in shallow water you will spook the bass.

To set up the rig use a four or six inch plastic worm on a number 1 or 1/0 wide gap hook. Add a 5/32 or 3/16 ounce brass bullet sinker and place a glass bead between the hook and the sinker. This will create a clicking noise when you shake your rod tip and will help in attracting bass. Some anglers also like to add some scent to the worm.

The type of worm you choose will depend on the type of water you are fishing and the season. Most anglers prefer paddle tail worms in the spring while straight tail worms are preferred in summer and fall. As far as color goes try crawdad in the spring but be aware that purple is the most popular color, especially on overcast days. In summer, motor oil is a hot color, and if you are fishing in stained water try red. On some waters blue and black can be hot colors. Along with plastic worms some anglers use grubs.

Once you get rigged up use your locator and drop your rig down to the level of the suspended bass. It is almost impossible to use the doodling technique without a fish locator since you will be feeling your way in the dark. When you are at the desired depth you want to fish, twitch the tip of your rod up and down with a sharp jerk in hopes of getting the attention of a suspended bass. If you don't detect a strike wait for a few seconds and then shake the rod tip for two or three seconds. Next pull the rod up about six inches and again let it drop back down to the level of the suspended bass. Keep repeating this technique until you catch a bass or decide that it's time to make a move. Before you make a move try slowing down your retrieve. The biggest mistake made by first time doodlers is they move the bait too fast.

Bites are rather subtle. If you feel a little weight and your line starts getting tight, set the hook. Since you are over open water it can't be a snag, therefore it must be a fish. In deep water the bite can feel more like a slight pull, like the pressure you feel when stretching a rubber band. Even if you feel anything "odd", set the hook! Don't set the hook too hard, an easy up swing will be sufficient if your hook is sharp. Always keep a file in your tackle box and periodically sharpen your hooks.

When doodling, it is critical to keep your presentation natural by downsizing your hooks and paying delicate, almost scrupulous attention to how straight your bait is in order to maintain a natural presentation. Most finesse worming is not a reaction strike so a worm that is not rigged properly will generally eliminate the possibility of ever hooking a bass. In addition, a long sweeping hook set will put the hook in the bass's mouth and keep it there more firmly than a fast hard hook-set. The sweep set will keep pressure, never allowing the hook to back out of the bass's mouth. It will also keep the bass deep until it has been played out. A fast hook-set will occasionally drop slack line and while you are trying to pick up the extra line a poorly hooked bass will drop the worm. A fast hook-set will also cause the bass to head for the surface and jump, which can result in a lost bass.

Bullet sinker, glass bead and worm

Most of my experience with doodling is on a stained water reservoir on the Menominee River. One summer day I was fishing alone, and instead of going to a spot where I knew I could catch a ton of smallmouth, when I launched the boat I headed in a different direction. Being a good guide, when I fish alone I will leave the honey hole for my clients and search for virgin fish and experiment with different presentations. That is what a guide does on his day off.

On this particular reservoir I will catch lots of smallmouth around a rip rap shoreline. By summer the big smallmouth move away from the rip rap and all that remains are small fish. When I fish the rip rap in summer we catch lots of smallmouth but seldom see fish over 17 inches. I would mark fish holding tight to the bottom in 25 feet of water, but I assumed that they were walleyes and never pursued them. I was determined to figure out where the big smallmouth were hiding and how to catch them. Since I was alone in the boat if I got skunked, it was no big deal.

The first place I stopped was a weedbed that dropped into 15 feet of water and intersected with the rip rap shoreline. I made several casts with a Case Sinking Minnow and eventually caught an 18 incher. By the time I fished the entire weedline I had boated 5 smallmouth and they were all over 17 inches. On my next pass I did not catch one smallmouth and it was evident they had either vacated the weeds or were just refusing my presentation.

I drifted off the weedline and watched my locator. As I drifted over 20 feet of water I noticed a large school of baitfish suspended at 12 feet below the surface. With my eyes glued on the locator I watched a school of large fish that seemed to be following the bait fish. Not wasting any time I tied on a deep diving crankbait and made a bunch of fan casts hoping to connect with whatever was chasing the baitfish. Well, that did not work and eventually I depleted all my resources and could not catch one fish.

Fortunately, for whatever the reason I remembered an article I had read about "Doodling" on clear water reservoirs. My situation seemed to parallel the article and so I decided to give it a try. The only problem was that in the article they were using six inch paddle tail and straight tail plastic worms. While I had brass bullet weights and beads in the boat most of my larger plastic worms were at home since I was loaded for river smallmouth. Knowing that I needed something that would be visual I decided to tie on a watermelon red four inch curly tail grub. On that particular reservoir I had caught both smallmouth and largemouth with that particular grub.

I rigged up the doodling rig and dropped it down to the suspended fish which I assumed were either largemouth or smallmouth bass. I tried a variety of different twitches and about the time I was ready to try something different I felt an odd pull on the end of the line. I knew enough to not set the hook hard and as I swept the rod upward I felt a fish throbbing on the end of the line. The fish headed straight down but I was in control and eventually heaved a big smallmouth into the boat. I gave the smallmouth a quick measurement and it easily pushed 20 inches. Needless to say, I was impressed; not so much with the size of the fish, but the fact that this doodling technique really worked.

Continuing to stay above the school of bass and keeping my four inch grub in the strike zone I caught four more smallmouth and all of them were over 17 inches. Finally, the school scattered and I lost contact with them. Deciding to move back to the weedline I continued to slowly work my doodling rig. Right at the breakline at the edge of the weeds where the weeds dropped to 20 feet of water I had another one of those odd pulls on the line. I again set the hook and instantly knew I had a good fish on the line. This time it was no big smallmouth but was instead a largemouth bass. Now the doodling rig really impressed me. I remained in the spot determined to catch another largemouth bass but there were none to be had.

The only problem I had the next day with my clients was in deciding whether to take them to my honey hole in the river or divulge my new technique. I opted to go up-river and we had an excellent day on the water. I guess that there are some things a guide just has to keep for himself. Occasionally I will try doodling not only in that spot but in similar locations. While I have caught nice bass, they just don't suspend much in these northern reservoirs.

On many of the small lakes that I fish, both largemouth and smallmouth bass suspend. Doodling seems to work on both species when the bass are suspended in the mid-depths of the water column. If bass are suspending high in the water column or off the bottom there are other presentations like drop shotting or fishing a grub that will catch more bass. However, if you see bass suspended in the mid-depths of the water column give doodling a try.

Rod manufacturers make rods designed specifically for doodling. While they come in both spinning and bait casting models, the typical rod is a 6 1/2 foot medium action. Most anglers spool their reels with six to eight pound test monofilament line but if the water is extremely clear four pound test gets the nod.

Like any presentation, fine tuning is critical to catching bass under all conditions and on all types of water. Many doodlers like to experiment with the beads. For example, there is a distinct difference in the sound emitted from a ceramic bead and a glass bead when it jars against the bullet sinker. Some anglers even use stainless steel beads. The color of the bead can have different reflectivity in the water and not attract bass and trigger a strike.

The position of the boat can also be an important aspect in doodling. In spring, a common practice is to fish uphill. In order to fish uphill you need to position the boat in shallow water and cast towards deep water. In fall, the best presentation is to fish downhill, positioning the boat in deep water and casting to shallow water.

If you are fishing clear water and the bite is light or non-existent, which is common, then downsize your plastics. When using a small worm keep slack in your line and barely shake the worm. Even a slight twitch of the rod can give a small worm amazing action.

Doodling is not for everyone and it is not meant to work on all waters. It is a presentation that takes time to perfect, but if you can master it, you will put more and bigger bass in the boat.

Chapter 12

Carolina Rigs

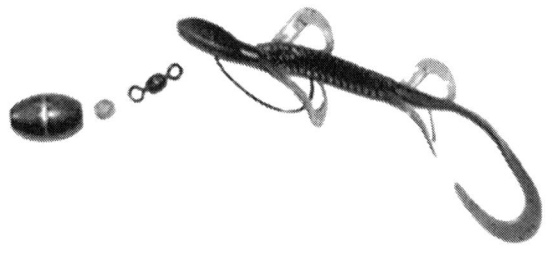

The Carolina rig is simple to rig, very efficient in producing bass, and uncomplicated to use. While all that sounds great, I often wonder why it seems to be a method of last resort, rather than the first choice of anglers. The multitude of rigging methods makes it versatile and it can be used in many situations in just about all kinds of water. Although it is a simple presentation to both use and rig up, it is most popular among experienced anglers and not the weekend warrior who could benefit from it immensely.

The debate about the history of the Carolina rig leads to controversy and uncertainty. While there is no documented proof of who developed the first Carolina rig, it appeared in the 1970's and it was originally called a swivel worm rig. When I first saw the Carolina rig, it looked like a modified version of a Lindy rig. The Lindy rig is drifted or trolled on the bottom with live bait and is used primarily for catching walleyes with live bait. At times I would target deep water smallmouth with Lindy rigs, tipping live bait hooks with leeches. I used the Lindy rig extensively and besides catching walleyes I caught both smallmouth and largemouth bass.

The question I often ask myself is, "Did some Yankee decide to drift a southern reservoir with a Lindy rig and start to catch bass?" Or, did some visiting southern angler see the Lindy rig and instead of using live bait decide to rig it with a plastic worm? I guess I will never know. One thing is for certain, the Carolina rig has its similarities to the Lindy rig. The Carolina rig is retrieved on the bottom with a plastic worm or plastic lizard. The concept is the same for both rigs: keep the sinker on the bottom and let the bait rise up off of the bottom.

The Carolina rig was originally developed for use in waters where the bottom is weedy. The idea being that you cast out and allow the weight to settle, while the soft lure rises above the weeds. You then feel the weight of the lure and allow a very small amount of slack line so that the lure rises a little more in the water. You can then twitch the lure and make it appear to be darting into the weed for cover from a predator. Generally, heavy sinkers are used, since this allows a person to work the lure without moving the weight itself. The lures used for Carolina rigging should be buoyant / floating types so that they will rise above the weeds on the bottom.

A Carolina rig separates the hook and worm from the sinker with a leader. To tie a rig, you slip a sinker on your line, follow it with one or two beads and then tie on a barrel swivel. The length of the leader should vary depending on the type of structure that will be fished. The type and size of hook that is tied onto the rig will be dictated by the size of the bait that you plan to use.

Depending on conditions, the lead can vary from $1/8^{th}$ of an ounce to one ounce and the leader can be from a few inches to six feet or more. The standard rig consists of a half-ounce sinker and a two foot leader. Generally, the clearer the water the longer the leader and the heavier the sinker should be. If the leader is too short or the sinker is too light, the rig will not stay on the bottom. A Carolina rig is one of the few exceptions to using light weights in clear water.

One of the best places to fish a Carolina rig is on long gravel points. Largemouth bass will relate to points during both the pre-spawn and post-spawn periods. The bass can scatter and a Carolina rig allows the angler to cover water quickly. By making a long cast and letting the rig fall to the bottom, the rig can be in the strike zone on the entire retrieve making it very deadly. It is the best method I know of for catching scattered bass.

A happy client with a largemouth bass caught on a Carolina Rig

I have used the Carolina rig successfully when fishing rocky points on clear water natural lakes during the post-spawn and early summer. The point needs to have a slow taper in order for the Carolina rig to work. If the point has sharp drop offs the sinker will either get hung up or the bait will drop too fast to be effective. When fishing a point for smallmouth I use a four inch ring worm or finesse worm.

In summer, a Carolina rig can also be deadly when working deep sand grass, although I prefer the Mojo rig which is similar but has the smaller cylindrical sinker. When using the Carolina rig for grass related smallmouth I prefer a four or six inch lizard or other creature baits like a brush hawg. Looking more like a mutant hybrid than any natural bait the Brush Hog sports appendages from head to toe. This gives a smallmouth more visual contact with the bait. I believe that the appendages also emit fish attracting vibration.

Another good place to fish a Carolina rig is around brush piles. A lethal tactic is to retrieve the rig to the brush pile and then stop. The worm or lizard will often draw a bass out of the brush pile. If that does not work, retrieve the sinker over the brush and let it fall, then stop the worm. The worm will sink slowly and will often be more than the bass can stand.

Carolina rigging has become a part of most serious bass anglers' arsenal with each angler having their personalized rigging method. Rod selection, reel preference, line selection, weight option, leader strength and length, whether to use beads or not and types of swivels can lead to intense dialogue among anglers.

The Carolina rig does have its limitations as to the type of cover in which you can fish it. Areas of dense weeds are the biggest problem for the Carolina rig. Even if the sinker slides through the weeds, the plastic baits and swivel will quickly become weed choked. In extreme rocky areas with large boulders the sinker will slide into a crevice and easily get hung up. Areas of dense brush can also be a problem. Along with determining the size of the weight, composition also plays a factor in selecting weights for the Carolina Rig. Lead has remained the most popular, but with recent environmental concerns as well as new developments in technology, it no longer remains the only choice. Brass is often utilized when fishing a Carolina Rig, given its ability to disseminate sound resembling a crawfish clacking its pincers together under water. Tungsten, on the other hand, provides not only extreme sensitivity but also, given its density, allows the sheer size of the weight (surface area) to be smaller compared to that of lead or brass.

The beads are an essential part of the Carolina rig and come in either plastic or glass. The glass beads are faceted, which means that they are not round, but have many flat sides to them. Usually there are two beads put onto the line after the sinker. Most anglers use the glass faceted. Some anglers think that using colored beads makes a difference, but it really comes down to personal choice. Using the two glass beads in line makes more of a clacker noise when the weight and the beads bang together, as opposed to the plastic beads.

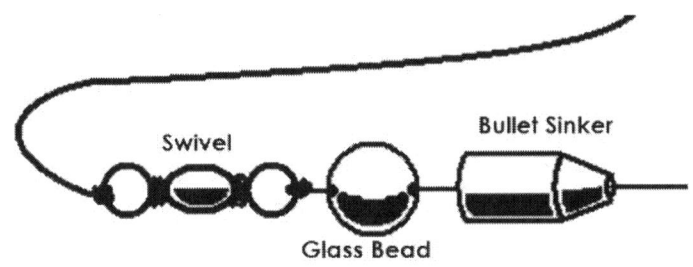

Carolina Rig with lizard

Adapting the Carolina rig to the mood of the bass is an important factor to consider when getting started. There are two main concepts in Carolina-rigging: Large baits and heavy tackle when bass are feeding, and smaller finesse baits/rigs on lighter tackle for fish that are more hesitant about eating. Most anglers will start out anticipating feeding bass and then switch to lighter rigs.

Power-fishing is a term often referred to when the bite is hot and bass are actively chasing prey. Bigger baits like a plastic lizard or crawfish will draw strikes from better quality fish. These conditions normally occur most often in stained water and during the summer when the water is warm. However, they can occur on any type of water during pre-frontal weather (overcast sky) which makes for ideal conditions for the larger baits.

When using larger baits, use a 7-foot medium-action bait casting rod and a reel spooled with 20-pound test line. Use a heavier 1-ounce bullet weight up the line followed with a two plastic beads and a brass two-way swivel. On the other end of the swivel tie a 4-7 ft. length of monofilament leader in 12- or 16-pound test. Next, add a 2/0 quality hook and thread on either a plastic lizard or crawfish. Try both baits to see which one the bass prefer. As a rule of thumb, if you are fishing around rocks use a crayfish and if you are fishing around wood or grass go with the lizard. However, never take anything for granted.

Regardless of which bait you choose, rig them with a "Tex-posed" hook, which is run completely through the body, then the exposed point is reinserted slightly into the plastic body. This will still make the bait weedless, but you don't have to pull the point all the way through the bait to set the hook,"

However, as most anglers know, on most days you won't experience a hot bite. If the bite is slow, I shift from the larger rig to a finesse rig, using the same Carolina concept, just downsized. I will make this adjustment when the water is clear, fishing pressure is heavy, a cold front has blown through (bright sky) or under any other condition that has bass off their feed.

When rigging for finesse presentations I use a 6-1/2 or 7-foot spinning rod and eight pound test line. I also go with two different rigs. In current, I'll stick with the 1 ounce sinker and the same swivel, but I'll change to a smaller leader, bait and hook. For instance, I'll use a 6-pound test leader, a #1 hook and a 4-inch Ring Worm or a 4 or 6 inch finesse worm. As far as beads go I use only one bead on my rig when the conditions call for a finesse presentation.

When even more finesse is needed, I will opt for a split-shot rig which offers an extra degree of subtlety. I'll use 8 pound test, and I'll peg a 3/16 or 1/8-ounce slip sinker a foot above my hook. Then I'll rig with a Ring Worm, a small finesse worm or a curly tail grub, and I'll drag this slowly across the bottom in up to 12 feet of water. This is a real good way to catch spooky bass on heavily pressured clear water lakes, or in summer when lakes are exploding with recreational boaters.

There are many other variations of the Carolina rig that are available to anglers if they choose to expand their arsenal; one is a tube bait rigged behind a light sinker. Insert a small piece of Styrofoam into the body of the tube so it will float up off the bottom. Another tactic is to push a chunk of Alka-Seltzer into the body so it will fizz and bubble during the retrieve. While I have never tried either one of these tactics, I know several anglers who have used them successfully.

Another variation is to use a floating minnow-imitation crankbait in place of plastics. An angler using this rig can fish a crankbait as deep as he wants, pulling then stopping the bait so it hangs tantalizingly in the strike zone. This tactic works best in clear water lakes but I have caught smallmouth while using this presentation in stained water reservoirs. This is a tactic that I have used successfully for both walleyes and bass with a Lindy Rig, long before I ever heard of a Carolina rig.

A floating crankbait used on a Carolina rig is very deadly when smallmouth are scattered on the deep edge of rocky points. When smallmouth are scattered off rocky points they usually suspend one to two feet off the bottom. Use your locator to establish the depth the smallmouth are suspending off the bottom and adjust the length of your leader accordingly. When adjusting your leader keep in mind that long is better than short. A smallmouth is more likely to move up to strike a bait and the longer the leader the higher the crankbait will float off the bottom.

While I have caught smallmouth with this technique in stained water, it is most deadly in clear water. The greater the water clarity the farther a smallmouth will travel to strike the crankbait. In dark water even the brightest colored crankbaits are not very effective. In clear water your crankbait color will depend on the conditions. When fishing under clear skies use crankbaits with reflectivity. Chrome and silver minnow imitation colors usually work the best. Under overcast conditions use black/white, blue/white and perch colored crankbaits. I use only rattling crankbaits on my Carolina Rigs. The noise created with the sinker and the beads is important when fishing plastics with the rattling crankbait adding more vibration.

All in all, the Carolina rig is an excellent choice when bass are staging off points, holding tight in the grass and scattered on the flats. It is no secret and I don't understand why it has not caught on in northern waters. Many northern lakes are heavily fished and it would be to an anglers' benefit to give a Carolina rig a try. This is a good presentation when all else seems to fail.

Chapter 13

Other Plastics

Pre-Rigged Worms

Some of the first plastic worms came pre-rigged with one to three or four hooks and the line threaded through the worm. They were a straight worm that had little if any action. While plastic worms have taken off in a variety of different directions, pre rigged worms were eventually made with a bend. The worms were hand poured, and with the hook harnesses inserted prior to pouring the worm it made the worm take on a cork screw appearance.

A pre-rigged plastic worm is made to be fished with a slow to medium speed due to its spiraling action. Most anglers just use the steady retrieve and rely on the spiraling action to attract the bass. With the three hooks, it does not matter how hard or where the fish hits the worm. All you need to do is set the hook with the slightest tug.

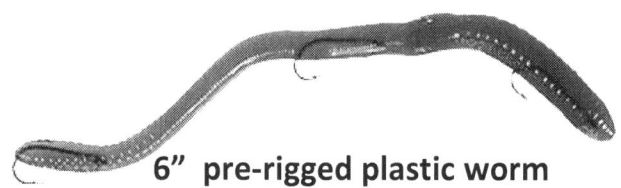
6" pre-rigged plastic worm

My favorite retrieve is a Start and Stop action. Do this by turning the reel handle 3 turns and then hesitating for a moment, then another 3 turns and hesitating and so on. Should you miss hooking the fish simply relax, let the worm settle for a few seconds, then start retrieving slowly while being ready to set the hook.

The use of a Snap-n-Swivel size 10 or 12 with a pre-rigged worm is necessary to help keep your line from twisting and will also add more action to the worm. If you wish to add more weight to a worm use one or two round split shot (size 3/0 or BB) just above the swivel. This will allow you to fish deeper and to fish at a faster rate of speed.

In the past I used pre-rigged worms in a similar manor that I use a wacky rigged soft plastic jerkbait today. Cast it tight to the shoreline and let it fall in the rocks. After it dropped to the bottom I would raise the worm and again let it fall. The three hooks make it a deadly bait for spawning bass.

Reaper Tails

One of the first things I learned when fishing northern waters for smallmouth bass is that they love leeches! Once the water temp hits 60 degrees, whether you are fishing in a river, reservoir or natural lake, if the fishing gets tough leeches will save the day. They are easy to use and can be fished on a plain hook or a jighead.

The closest thing to an artificial leech is a reaper tail. Reaper tails are also popular with walleye, pike and muskie fishermen and a few manufacturers make them up to 8 inches. However, most smallmouth anglers use reapers in the three and four inch size.

My favorite method for fishing a three inch reaper tail is to rig it on a $1/16^{th}$ or $1/8^{th}$ darter head jig. The long shank and small head will allow the reaper tail to look as natural as possible. Cast out the jig and reaper letting it drop a few feet, then use a slow steady retrieve. On occasion I will let the jig drop but only for a few seconds before continuing my retrieve. When you feel a pick up wait a few seconds and set the hook. If the smallmouth are hugging the bottom on the flats or along rocky shorelines I will rig the reaper tail on a 1/0 wide gape hook with the hook Tex-posed.

I have not had much success fishing reaper tails on shoreline points but they are dynamite on off shore humps. I will fish the reaper on a darter head jig when looking for smallmouth suspended off the hump. When smallmouth are tight to the bottom, rig the reaper tail on a stand-up jighead.

Reaper tails are also an excellent bait for working deep weedlines for largemouth bass. For weedline bass I prefer a four or five inch reaper rigged on a stand-up jighead. Use a heavy enough stand-up jighead to allow the jig and reaper to sink to the bottom. The most popular method is to crawl the jig along the bottom keeping as close to the weedline as possible. I like to stop the jig occasionally and hop it a few times. A bass will follow the jig and hit it on the fall of the hop.

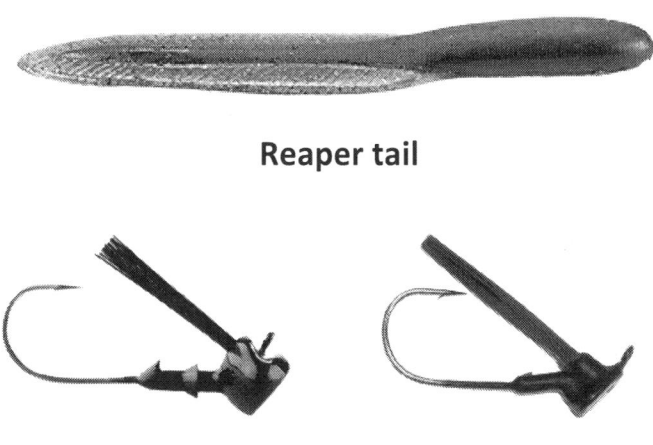

Reaper tail

Stand up jig heads

Another option is to retrieve the reaper and stand up jighead at various levels in the water column. While the stand-up jighead will work, I prefer a Tex-pose 1/0 or 2/0 wide gap hook with a worm weight pegged in front of the reaper. I don't know if people use this in southern waters, but on northern lakes it is deadly for largemouth bass. While there are many color reaper tails available all I ever use is black. I guess it gets back to my faith in leeches.

Creature Baits

Recent years have seen an entirely new lure type, "creature baits," become increasingly popular among bass fishermen. In fact, there are literally hundreds of models on the market today. Creature baits are perfect for fishing murky or deep water because their moving appendages create more water displacement than other soft plastics, but they're also a good choice when fishing for bedded bass. Fished on a Texas-rig, a Carolina-rig, a jighead or a jig trailer, this bait broke the mold on standard plastics. Before this bait, soft plastics had to resemble some sort of creature that existed in the water. Anglers used lizards, craws, worms, tubes and grubs.

Brush Hawg

Case Brush Puppie

The creature creation of Ed Chambers sent soft plastic manufacturers in new directions realizing you could impart a lot more action and water displacement with baits that didn't have to resemble a real creature. After the brush hawg however there was an explosion of soft plastics that didn't resemble anything.

In recent years, Beaver-style baits have also become popular. In sparse weeds, Texas rig a creature bait with a 1/4 oz. pegged sinker. In denser mats of milfoil and water chestnut, use a heavier weight to poke through the vegetation. Creature baits are very effective for smallmouth and largemouth when fished with a Carolina rig.

Another creature style bait that will catch loads of bass is the sweet beaver. The sweet beaver fishes like a tube because it falls with a similar gliding action but imitates a crawfish or, even, a baitfish. The advantage with the sweet beaver it that there is no way, no matter if it's upside down or sideways, that you can mess it up. It's a 100-percent perfect pitching and flipping bait. It falls almost perfectly every time. Other soft plastics, creature baits and tubes, can get fouled easily with a piece of grass, or hit a branch the wrong way, thus messing up the presentation.

You can also put the sweet beaver on the back of jigs for a jig-n-pig look. When using the sweet beaver with a jig many bass anglers break the tail. It's pretty easy to split because there's only two tiny pieces holding the middle together. However, if you split the tail the bait will have a different action.

**A sweet beaver rigged on a jighead
is a great smallmouth bait**

Chunk Trailers

For years, there was really no alternative for anglers who liked to fish a jig for bass. They either fished it bare, or tipped it with a pork chunk. That made Uncle Josh almost a household world in the bass-fishing community, because so many fishermen owned jars and jars of the fatback/pork rind. Used even more was the term "jig n' pig" to denote a rubber-skirted jig fished with an Uncle Josh pork frog.

Soft Plastics For Bass

But in the mid-1990s, companies that made plastic worms, lizards and crawfish saw a niche in the fishing market. Could they make a chunk of plastic that resembled an old, original pork-frog chunk, and would bass bite it the way they do pork? They made the chunks and, apparently, bass like them, because a lot of companies that make plastic worms now have a plastic chunk among their line of products.

What is better, "Pork or Plastic"? Most admit that plastic chunks will do everything a pork chunk will do under most circumstances, without the fuss and mess of dealing with slimy pork chunks and the jars and lids that never seem to want to come off. However, many anglers including myself feel that pork chunks have a natural, built-in action that plastic can't imitate. A pork chunk swims better than a plastic chunk; it has more action and it floats better.

Most anglers feel that plastic chunks work well for their style of bass fishing. Plastic chunks can cover the hook point when a bass inhales it, thereby making for a poor hookset that occasionally drives the point into the chunky plastic rather than into the fish's mouth. Another disadvantage is that most anglers imbed plastic chunks onto the hook in the same manner that they hook a pork chunk, thereby making it easy for a bass to rip the chunk off the hook when the bass bite light.

Zoom Trailer

Case Salt Trailer

Charlies Chunk Trailer

One day a client of mine who fished with a bass guide in southern waters showed me a trick to help eliminate the bass from ripping the pork chunk off the hook. You insert a short piece of a toothpick into the chunky part in front of the point where the hook sits in the chunk. In this way, it is not so easy for a bass to tear off the chunk, but it still can fold over and facilitate a good hookset. See, on occasion a guide can learn a tip from a client!

Another option for rigging a plastic pork chunk is to thread the chunk onto the shank of the hook just like you would rig up a plastic worm. Start rigging the chunk front and center like you would with soft plastics but take the hook out of the top of the chunk once it has penetrated about ½ inch. The chunk should still sit well back on the hook shank, just before the bend starts. Make sure it lies fairly flat or is even pointing slightly upwards. Next, slide it back up, put a shot of superglue on the hook shank where the plastic chunk will sit and slide it back down into place. Once dry the chunk will stay in place without getting torn off.

Made in the USA
Lexington, KY
17 October 2016